JOSH MOSEY
BOB EVENHOUSE

3-MINUTE DEVOTIONS

BOLD MEN OF FAITH

180

CHALLENGING
READINGS

BARBOUR
PUBLISHING

Previously released as *Men of Valor: 3-Minute Devotions*

© 2020 by Barbour Publishing, Inc.

ISBN 978-1-63609-734-3

Cover Design: Greg Jackson, Thinkpen Design

Published by Barbour Publishing, Inc., 1810 Barbour Drive, Uhrichsville, Ohio 44683, www.barbourbooks.com

Our mission is to inspire the world with the life-changing message of the Bible.

Member of the
Evangelical Christian
Publishers Association

Printed in China.

To DeAnne, who encourages and prays for me to be a man of valor. J. M.
To Cindy, my love. I'd want no one else with me during this grand adventure. B. E.

INTRODUCTION

Bravery can be carrying an injured comrade through live fire on a battlefield. Or it could be speaking up for someone who's been treated unfairly. Or it might even be holding fast to God's Word when the rest of the world seems actively antagonistic.

Bold men of faith do brave, selfless things—and the world is better for them. Now, here are 180 brief readings based on the lives of courageous Christian men, offering examples and insights for your own life of faith. Within these pages, you'll be guided through just-right-size readings that you can experience in as few as three minutes:

- Minute 1: Reflect on God's Word
- Minute 2: Read real-life stories and applications
- Minute 3: Pray, with the prayer starter provided

From Augustine to Dietrich Bonhoeffer, from Frederick Douglass to Billy Graham, here are glimpses of the valorous lives of thirty-one memorable men of faith. Each one demonstrates how complete commitment to God makes a man bold—and accomplishes great things in this world.

Take three minutes to read and pray, and see how God will build valor in your own life. The world will be better for you!

Be on guard.
Stand firm in the faith.
Be courageous.
Be strong.
1 CORINTHIANS 16:13 NLT

GOD'S CALLING FIRST

*"But seek first his kingdom and his righteousness,
and all these things will be given to you as well."*
MATTHEW 6:33 NIV

When you hear the name Dietrich Bonhoeffer, you may think of his books: *The Cost of Discipleship*, *Life Together*, or others. You might also recall his open opposition to Adolf Hitler and the Nazi party during World War II. Would you be surprised to learn that he grew up in a nonreligious family? Or that he was an immensely talented musician before he even reached his teen years?

Dietrich's family was disappointed when he announced—at the age of fourteen—that he intended to become a minister. This decision to follow Christ, instead of what his family believed best, put Bonhoeffer on a path that would impact thousands of lives. . .and eventually cost him his life.

That's the kind of wholehearted devotion that God honors. As the Lord told the prophet Jeremiah, "You will seek me and find me when you seek me with all your heart" (29:13 NIV).

Following God, no matter what the world says, is always the best and most honorable path for your life.

*Father, help me to focus on Your path for my
life, no matter what others want me to do.*

GOD'S PURPOSES PREVAIL

*When Jesus reached the spot, he looked up
and said to him, "Zacchaeus, come down
immediately. I must stay at your house today."*
LUKE 19:5 NIV

Andrew van der Bijl was born May 11, 1928, into a God-fearing home in the Netherlands. Although he gained fame as Brother Andrew, the audacious Bible smuggler, he was not always a relentless champion of the Word of God.

During his youth, Andrew often grew bored during church. He longed for the outdoors and adventure more than Jesus. Even when his country was invaded by the Nazi war machine, Brother Andrew did not turn to faith—instead, he found purpose in the Dutch Resistance. Still, he kept his mother's Bible with him all through the war.

Sometimes, the stories of Christian heroes contain elements we might not expect. An individual might be far from God, but an encounter with the living Christ can change that. And, as with Jesus' calling of Zacchaeus, that experience is a springboard to bigger and better things—perhaps even a lifetime of sharing the gospel with the world.

---

*Father, I know my heart will wander at
times. Please send people into my life who
will encourage me toward Your will.*

SOLDIER SAVED BY GRACE

*But because of his great love for us, God, who
is rich in mercy, made us alive with Christ
even when we were dead in transgressions—
it is by grace you have been saved.*
EPHESIANS 2:4–5 NIV

Though remembered as author of *The Pilgrim's Progress*, John Bunyan was more than an early English writer. He was a sinner saved by grace.

Bunyan was born in 1628 in Bedfordshire, England. His father was a tinker—someone who made and repaired objects like pots, pans, and utensils—who taught his trade to John. At the age of sixteen, in the same year that his mother and sister died, John enlisted in the Parliamentary army. He would serve for three years.

Once, a fellow soldier asked John to swap places for an upcoming action. In his book *Grace Abounding*, Bunyan wrote of that soldier who, "as he stood sentinel, he was shot in the head with a musket-bullet and died."

John Bunyan was spared when someone took his place. He later recognized that God's grace had preserved him for another purpose. . .and over hundreds of years, countless people have benefited from John Bunyan's spiritual insights.

*Lord, thank You for taking my place
like the soldier who took John Bunyan's.
Please set me apart for Your purposes.*

COURSE CORRECTION

> *May your hand be ready to help me,*
> *for I have chosen your precepts.*
> PSALM 119:173 NIV

John Calvin was born in 1509 in France, a staunch Catholic nation. His family was deeply devoted to Catholicism, and at age twelve, John began to serve as chaplain at the Cathedral of Noyon. He was destined for a career in the church.

Today, though, John Calvin is not remembered for his work in the Catholic Church. He is known as a cornerstone of the Reformation, a movement that arose as a counterpoint to the faith in which he was raised.

John Calvin followed in the footsteps of Martin Luther, becoming a champion of the Protestant beliefs that impacted Christianity worldwide. To leave such a legacy, he had to forgo the career planning of his father and the religion of his own country.

Can you imagine making such choices in order to pursue God's calling for your life? John Calvin probably never guessed how influential his course correction would be.

What about you? Do you sense God nudging you to make a life change today?

> *Father, no matter what crossroads I encounter,*
> *may I always seek Your will first.*

AN EDUCATION IN PERSEVERANCE

*You need to persevere so that when you have done the
will of God, you will receive what he has promised.*
HEBREWS 10:36 NIV

Born in 1761 in the village of Paulerspery, England, William Carey converted to the faith while working as an apprentice in a cobbler shop.

From the beginning, he took up his Christianity with great dedication. Although uneducated, he devoted himself to learning the original languages of the Bible—Greek and Hebrew—as well as Latin.

While William Carey's spiritual life flourished, he endured great struggle in his family and career. He married and had a child, who died at age two. His cobbler apprentice's pay wasn't enough to support his family, so they lived in poverty. But William Carey's faithfulness never wavered. "I can plod," he wrote. "I can persevere to any definite pursuit."

How is your life right now? Are some areas flourishing while others are stagnant. . .or worse? As Christians we are called to be faithful, even when our life circumstances aren't everything we'd hope for. Today, identify one difficult aspect of life and commit to perseverance. Like William Carey, you can plod!

*Father, fill with me faithfulness and
joy even when life is challenging.*

RANSOMED SLAVE

I will shout for joy and sing your praises,
for you have ransomed me.
PSALM 71:23 NLT

Before he became the first African American to attend and then teach at Iowa State University, before he was recognized for his contributions to farming, before *Time* magazine called him a "Black Leonardo," George Washington Carver was a slave. He was born near Diamond, Missouri, a few years before slavery was abolished in 1865.

One week after his birth, night raiders kidnapped George, his sister, and his mother. Their owners, Moses and Susan Carver, hired a man to find them, but he was only able to track down George. Moses paid for the baby's return by giving up his finest racehorse. When slavery was abolished, the Carvers raised George as a son, teaching him to read and write.

George Washington Carver's early experience is astounding but has a familiar ring for Christians. Everyone is born into the slavery of sin, and we are only freed because Jesus' sacrifice has paid our ransom. Now we are welcomed into God's family, raised to grow in our knowledge of Him and His love.

Lord, thank You for ransoming me from
sin. Help me live in freedom for You.

FREEDOM IN CHRIST

*"Come to me, all you who are weary and
burdened, and I will give you rest."*
MATTHEW 11:28 NIV

During all the years of legalized slavery in America, few abolitionists were as impactful as Frederick Douglass. He became a confidant of Presidents Lincoln and Johnson, as well as a prominent supporter of women's rights.

Douglass came from humble beginnings. He was born in a slave cabin and never knew his white father. Raised by his grandparents for six years, he was ultimately sent to Baltimore.

There, Frederick Douglass learned to read, sometimes swapping food with other children for grammar lessons. He also encountered the African Methodist Episcopal Church and a Christianity much different than the proslavery "gospel" he had known his entire life.

This revelation initially frightened Frederick Douglass, who wondered if he could really trust Christ. But he soon gave his life to Jesus and found a "Redeemer, Savior and Friend."

Is anything blocking your full acceptance of Jesus today? Can you—like Frederick Douglass—take your burdens to Christ and find rest?

*Father, here is my heart. Take all of it. I lay my sin
at your feet and place my hope in Your salvation.*

YALE AT AGE TWELVE

For the LORD giveth wisdom: out of his mouth
cometh knowledge and understanding.
PROVERBS 2:6 KJV

The only son of eleven children, Jonathan Edwards was born in 1703 with ministry in his blood. His father, Timothy Edwards was a minister in East Windsor, Connecticut and his maternal grandfather was the Reverend Solomon Stoddard of Northampton, Massachusetts. After a solid education at home, Jonathan entered the Collegiate School of Connecticut at age twelve.

A few years after Jonathan began his formal education, the school changed its name to honor a generous donor, becoming Yale College. Edwards flourished at Yale, embracing the studies of science and God with equal abandon. Though he was gifted academically, he wasn't prideful of his education.

Later in life, Edwards wrote, "Seek not to grow in knowledge chiefly for the sake of applause, and to enable you to dispute with others; but seek it for the benefit of your souls."

God wants you to learn and study too—not for your own glory, but for His. Whether you attended Yale at age twelve or you dropped out of elementary school, learn! The desire for knowledge will inevitably lead you to the source of all truth: God.

Lord, help me be a good student,
eager to learn more about You.

EVERY MORNING WITH GOD

I delight in your decrees; I will not neglect your word.
PSALM 119:16 NIV

Jim Elliot was only twenty-eight when he was martyred by an indigenous Ecuadorian tribe. He and four friends lost their lives attempting to share the gospel with the hostile Waodani people. Although famous for this encounter, Jim's story started thousands of miles away in Portland, Oregon, where he was born in 1927 to Christian parents. Jim came to know Jesus at the age of six.

Although an adventure lover, Jim's foundation of faith came from self-discipline, including regular time in the Bible. He wrote of the essential daily practice of scripture reading, "None of it gets to be 'old stuff' for it is Christ in print, the Living Word. We wouldn't think of rising in the morning without a face-wash, but we often neglect the purgative cleansing of the Word of the Lord. It wakes us up to our responsibility."

What do you think of the Bible? Is it simply a rulebook to obey or the living Word of God? Is anything keeping you from incorporating the life-giving scripture into your daily routine?

Father, root Your Word in my heart.
Help me search for time to connect with You.

FROM RAGS TO HEAVENLY RICHES

*Therefore if any man be in Christ, he is a
new creature: old things are passed away;
behold, all things are become new.*
2 CORINTHIANS 5:17 KJV

Born in 1829 to a working-class English family, William Booth had a humble entrance into the world. Eighty-three years later, his funeral was attended by 150,000 people—even the Queen of England paid her respects. A long road of faith led William Booth from obscurity to founding the Salvation Army to his ultimate promotion to glory.

Too poor to attend school, working as a pawnbroker's assistant to support his family, William knew destitution. At age fifteen, though, the trajectory of his life shifted when he put his faith in Jesus Christ. In his diary, he wrote, "God shall have all there is of William Booth." Almost immediately, he began to evangelize to the poor and needy.

Salvation remade William Booth. His actions, motivations, and plans changed because of his commitment to Christ.

Today, does God have all there is of you? When you commit fully to Him, you may not expect large crowds to attend your funeral—but you'll have crowns of your own to offer to God in glory.

Lord, take all of me. Change my plans to be Yours.

EVANGELIST TO THE WORLD

*And then he told them, "Go into all the world
and preach the Good News to everyone."*
MARK 16:15 NLT

It would be difficult to find a more famous evangelist than Billy Graham. From the time of his first evangelistic "crusade" in 1947 until his death in 2018, he seemed to be everywhere. Graham preached the gospel in person to nearly 215 million people in more than 185 countries and territories.

Not only was he famous, Billy Graham was well liked. At the time of his death, he had appeared on Gallup's list of "Most Admired Men" sixty-one times, more than anyone else since the annual poll began in 1948.

For all his fame, Billy Graham was simply a country boy who answered God's call. And God blessed his ministry.

Many have asked who the next Billy Graham will be. According to Billy, it could be *you*. "When God gets ready to shake America, he may not take the Ph.D. and the D.D. God may choose a country boy," he said. "God may choose the man that no one knows, a little nobody, to shake America for Jesus Christ in this day, and I pray that He would!"

*Lord, I'm answering Your call.
Use me to spread the gospel.*

LITERATURE AND CHRIST

*Listen, my son, to your father's instruction and
do not forsake your mother's teaching.*
PROVERBS 1:8 NIV

C. S. Lewis was one of the most influential Christian thinkers of
the twentieth century. He is the author of many books including
Mere Christianity, *The Screwtape Letters*, and the Chronicles of
Narnia series. Although deeply entrenched in the academic world,
his great writing skill enabled him to reach scholars, lay Christians,
and children. Lewis taught at Oxford University and was a founding
member of the famed writers' group "the Inklings."

Clive Staples Lewis was born in Belfast, Ireland, on November
29, 1898. His parents were devout members of the Church of
Ireland who loved books. As a child, Lewis was saturated with
literature; he wrote in his autobiography that books were piled
in every room of his childhood home.

Though C. S. Lewis would go through periods of spiritual doubt
and even atheism before returning to his parents' faith, there is
no doubt that their love for God and literature left an indelible
impression on him. What kind of impression are you making on
the world around you?

*Father, I want to know You personally so I can leave a
powerful impression of You on the people around me.*

TWO GOOD OPTIONS

*The LORD makes firm the steps
of the one who delights in him.*
PSALM 37:23 NIV

Eric Liddell was born to missionary parents in Tientsin (now Tianjin), China, in 1902. He would become famous half a world away as the sprinter who won the 400-meter Olympic gold medal in the 1924 Olympics.

Originally, Eric Liddell planned to compete in the 100-meter race, but since the event was scheduled on a Sunday, he refused to compete and opted for a longer race later in the week. His story was immortalized in the Oscar-winning 1981 film *Chariots of Fire*.

At age six, Eric was sent to a boarding school for missionary children. From there, he would go on to join his brother Rob at Edinburgh University. Eric excelled in rugby and running, earning international acclaim for each. Since there wasn't enough time to focus on both sports along with his studies, Eric focused on running.

Sometimes life presents us with two good options, and our job is to decide which one God wants us to pursue. We can pray for His wisdom, and trust that He will direct our steps toward the future best suited for His kingdom.

Father, thank You for always directing my steps.

David Livingstone

WHEN PLANS CHANGE

*The Lord is not slow in keeping his promise,
as some understand slowness. Instead he is
patient with you, not wanting anyone to perish,
but everyone to come to repentance.*
2 PETER 3:9 NIV

David Livingstone has towns, roads, and buildings named for him in Africa, Europe, and both American continents. He was awarded the gold medal of the Royal Geographical Society of London and referred to as "Africa's Greatest Missionary."

Born March 19, 1813, Livingstone grew up in Blantyre, Scotland. At age ten, he worked twelve-hour days at a cotton mill. Having spent his youth indoors, it isn't surprising that he'd be drawn in later years to explore nature.

As a young man, he read an appeal for medical missionaries in China and convinced his family that he should become a doctor. But when his training was complete, the door to China was closed. The door to Africa though, was wide open.

When our plans change, we must remember that God's plan hasn't. With China out of the picture, Livingstone could have opened a medical practice in his homeland of Scotland—but he followed God's leading to Africa. When your expectations don't work out, watch for the "alternate" plan. . .the one that was probably God's plan all along.

---

*Lord, Your plans do not change.
Change mine to look like Yours.*

LAWYER VS. LIGHTNING

> *Listen, I tell you a mystery: We will not all sleep,*
> *but we will all be changed—in a flash, in the*
> *twinkling of an eye, at the last trumpet.*
> 1 CORINTHIANS 15:51–52 NIV

Martin Luther—Reformation hero, writer of hymns, scandalously married priest—was almost a lawyer.

Born in 1483, he was the eldest of several siblings in a family whose livelihood came from copper mining. His father, Hans, determined that his son should have a better life than himself, pushed Martin toward a career in law.

Martin received his master's degree in 1505. But in July of that year, while riding a horse during a thunderstorm, lightning struck close by.

"Help! Saint Anna, I will become a monk!" he cried. Faced with death and divine judgment, he wanted to be more than a lawyer. Martin sold his books (angering his father) and entered Saint Augustine's Monastery.

In time, he would discover the grace that set his soul free. If you have too—if you know that Jesus died for your sins and believe that God raised Him from the dead—your soul is safe. It doesn't matter if you're a lawyer, a preacher, or a jockey.

Lord, I accept Your free gift of salvation.
Thank You for grace!

SHOE SALESMAN

*As it is written: "How beautiful are the feet
of those who bring good news!"*
ROMANS 10:15 NIV

Dwight Lyman Moody was born in 1837. At age seventeen, with only a fifth-grade education and some farming experience, he left home for Boston where he asked for a job in his uncle's shoe store. Uncle Samuel hired D. L. on the condition that he attend Mt. Vernon Congregational Church.

At Mt. Vernon, Moody was placed in Edward Kimball's Sunday school class. The teacher later visited D. L. at the shoe store and led him to Christ in the back room.

Kimball later said, "I have seen few persons whose minds were spiritually darker than was his when he came into my Sunday school class; and I think that the [church] seldom met an applicant for membership more unlikely ever to become a Christian of clear and decided views of gospel truth, still less to fill any extended sphere of public usefulness."

The church was wrong about D. L. Moody, whom God used to reach countless thousands of people. God can use anyone— regardless of their past or reputation—if he will allow himself to be used.

---

*Lord, when people doubt me, prove Your
power and grace through me.*

PRINCE KABOO

> *If the Son therefore shall make you*
> *free, ye shall be free indeed.*
> JOHN 8:36 KJV

Born around 1873, he would come to be known as Samuel Morris. But until that time, he was Prince Kaboo of the Kru tribe in Africa.

At age eleven, Kaboo was kidnapped by the rival Grebo tribe and held in exchange for the Kru's ivory, palm nuts, and India rubber. Although the prince's father paid the ransom monthly, his captors declared each offering insufficient, keeping both the goods and Kaboo.

While in Grebo hands, the prince was whipped mercilessly and regularly. During one whipping session, Kaboo saw a light flash from heaven and heard a voice tell him to flee. The ropes fell from his hands, and he ran for the jungle, escaping from the Grebo tribe.

In many ways, Kaboo's life pictures the Christian's experience. Sin holds us captive, and our own efforts to pay ransom come up short. But God sends a light from heaven—Jesus—and tells us to flee. We are free from our sins! They have no power over us because Jesus Christ has power over them.

> *Lord may I live in the freedom You paid for.*
> *Help me escape every bondage to sin in my life.*

ACCEPTING THE INVITATION

Open your mouth wide, and I will fill it with good things.
PSALM 81:10 NLT

You may know that George Müller oversaw a ministry to British orphans in the nineteenth century. You may also have heard that those orphans were miraculously provided for, as God answered Müller's direct, no-nonsense prayers that took the Lord at His word. Today's verse is a key aspect of George Müller's story.

Concerned about the plight of needy kids, Müller was stirred to establish an orphanage. But he had an even higher goal, that of giving the church "visible proof of the unchangeable faithfulness of the Lord." One day, as Müller read Psalm 81:10, the verse jumped out at him. "If I, a poor man, simply by prayer and faith obtained, without asking any individual, the finances for establishing and carrying on an orphan house, this might strengthen the faith of the children of God."

He was right about that—Christians have marveled at George Müller's example for well over a century. Today, God offers each of us the same invitation. Open your mouth wide, and allow Him to fill it with good things.

Lord God, give me the boldness to take You at Your word. Inspire me to ask for big things that meet needs.

LIGHT IN THE DARK

"I prayed for this child, and the LORD has granted me what I asked of him. So now I give him to the LORD."
1 SAMUEL 1:27–28 NIV

Nee Shu-tsu (English name, Henry Nee) was born in Foochow, China, in 1903. His mother, who'd birthed two daughters, had asked God for a son. When Henry was born, she dedicated him to the Lord just as the biblical Hannah did with Samuel. Unlike Samuel, it took seventeen years for Henry to give his life to God. Until that time, he was solely focused on his education, finishing at the top of each of his classes.

When he did commit himself to Jesus, Henry felt called to carry out the Great Commission. He changed his name from "Henry" to "Watchman"—in Chinese, from Nee Shu-tsu to To-sheng, meaning "the sound of a watchman's rattle." He wanted to be a warning bell in the dark night of his world.

A century later, our world is just as dark—if not darker. Can you be a watchman to your friends and family, sharing the good news of Jesus Christ? Today, think of one person who needs to know Jesus, and ask God to give you an opportunity to share.

Father, empower me to be a light and shine for Christ to the world around me.

LOVE OR IDOLATRY

> *Husbands, love your wives, even as Christ also*
> *loved the church, and gave himself for it.*
> EPHESIANS 5:25 KJV

John Newton was born in 1725. His mother died when he was six, and he was raised by his father, an irreligious shipmaster. By the time John was seventeen, plans were made for him to work at a sugarcane plantation in Jamaica. A chance encounter in Kent, though, changed everything—John met his future wife.

"Almost at the first sight of this girl (for she was then under fourteen), I was impressed with an affection for her," he recalled, "which never abated or lost its influence a single moment in my heart."

To be near his new love, John deliberately overstayed his visit and missed the ship for Jamaica. His affection stirred action, but not necessarily right living. In fact, Newton compared it to idolatry, saying, "it greatly weakened my sense of religion, and made farther way for the entrance of infidel principles."

Newton would later be powerfully saved and write the classic hymn "Amazing Grace." But his early life provides a warning for us: Do we truly love others? Always remember that true love seeks to benefit the other person. Beyond that is idolatry.

> *Lord, may I love sacrificially like You,*
> *instead of making idols of my affection.*

SUMMER CAMP CONVERT

If you declare with your mouth, "Jesus is Lord,"
and believe in your heart that God raised
him from the dead, you will be saved.
ROMANS 10:9 NIV

Luis Palau Jr. shared the gospel with millions through his worldwide evangelistic crusades. Some of the credit for that goes to Frank Chandler, a summer camp counselor who led the twelve-year-old Palau to Christ in 1947.

Though he grew up attending Sunday school and heard about Christ at the missionary-run boarding school he attended, Luis was unsure of his salvation. That changed when he attended summer camp.

Each night, Frank would rouse a boy from bed, lead him beneath the stars, and present him with the gospel. On the last night of camp, Luis knew what was coming. When he feigned sleep to avoid the conversation, Frank dumped him off his mattress and took him outside. It was beginning to rain, so the conversation was quick—but soon Luis confessed Jesus as Lord.

Thank God for people like Frank Chandler, who persist in sharing the gospel even when we pretend to be asleep. Thank God for His pursuit of us when we were dead in our sins!

Lord, give me the courage to follow You
when I'd rather pretend to be asleep.

THE POWER OF SCRIPTURE

The unfolding of your words gives light;
it gives understanding to the simple.
PSALM 119:130 NIV

When you hear the name Saint Augustine, who do you think of? An early church leader, writer of *Confessions*, or maybe that he was at one time the bishop of Hippo? What might surprise you is that Augustine did not convert to the Christian faith until he was thirty-two years old.

Before he confessed Jesus as Lord, he tried intellectual pursuits in hopes of understanding life. He also struggled with sexual sin and even had a concubine with whom he fathered a son.

In his *Confessions*, Augustine relates the almost mystical story of hearing a child's voice repeating, "Take up and read! Take up and read!" Feeling this a command from God, Augustine opened the scripture and read "put ye on the Lord Jesus Christ, and make not provision for the flesh" (Romans 13:14 KJV). He was quickly converted.

Time with the Bible can be life changing. Have you read yours yet today?

Father, may I never forget the importance of Your Word,
the Bible. Help me to read and study it regularly.

LOOK UNTO ME

*Look unto me, and be ye saved, all the ends of the
earth: for I am God, and there is none else.*
ISAIAH 45:22 KJV

Born in Essex in 1834 as the son of a Nonconformist minister, Charles Spurgeon was no stranger to Christianity—but his conversion didn't happen until age fifteen. That's when a snowstorm forced him to seek shelter in a Primitive Methodist church, where he heard the salvation message with new ears. Charles Spurgeon finally gave his life to Christ.

"I have heard men tell the story of their conversion, and of their spiritual life, in such a way that my heart hath loathed them and their story, too," wrote Spurgeon, "for they have told of their sins as if they did boast in the greatness of their crime, and they have mentioned the love of God, not with a tear of gratitude, not with the simple thanksgiving of the really humble heart, but as if they as much exalted themselves as they exalted God."

Is your testimony more about yourself? Or do you know in your deepest heart that salvation begins and ends with the Lord? Thankfulness and praise are always the appropriate response to His great grace.

*Lord, I humbly thank You for the gift of salvation.
Turn my eyes back to You if they drift toward myself.*

FROM FIELD TO FAITH

Who shall separate us from the love of Christ?
Shall trouble or hardship or persecution or
famine or nakedness or danger or sword?
ROMANS 8:35 NIV

William Ashley Sunday was born in a log cabin near Ames, Iowa in 1862. This was during the American Civil War, and Billy's father served in a local volunteer infantry. He died from pneumonia when Billy was just five weeks old.

Hardship would mark most of the boy's early life. His mother struggled financially, and when her son was ten, he was sent to an orphan's home for soldiers' children in Davenport, Iowa. There, Billy learned discipline, gained an education, and discovered his incredible affinity for and ability in baseball.

In 1883, Billy reached the major leagues, playing for the Chicago White Stockings. In Chicago one day, Billy heard a street corner sermon by a team from the Pacific Garden Mission. Hymns that Billy recalled from childhood drew him back to the mission for more sermons. Soon he gave his life to Christ, and he would go on to become a renowned evangelist.

Are you experiencing tough times in your life right now? Trust that your heavenly Father is working in the background for His purposes, and your good.

Father, create in me a heart steadfastly
devoted to You in good times and bad.

ZEAL FOR CHINA

Declare his glory among the nations,
his marvelous deeds among all peoples.
1 CHRONICLES 16:24 NIV

James and Amelia Taylor welcomed their son into the world in 1832. As they held little Hudson, they prayed that he would work for the Lord in a place that fascinated them, China.

As Hudson grew, he departed from his parents' faith and wandered away from God. But by age seventeen, his parent's prayer would be answered: Hudson came to Christ through the reading of a gospel tract. After reading a book about China borrowed from a friend, Hudson began studying Mandarin, Greek, Hebrew, and Latin. His heart was set on serving in the very country his parents prayed that he would.

Once he committed his life to Jesus, Hudson Taylor was all in. His recreation, the books he read, and the subjects he studied were focused on one thing: preparing him for service in China.

How about you? Are you "all in" for Jesus? He wants your full commitment, but He also provides the power for it. Just ask Him. . .He knows exactly what you need.

Lord God, I want to be fully committed to You.
Please guide and strengthen me in Your way.

LOVING GOD'S WORD

Thy word have I hid in mine heart,
that I might not sin against thee.
PSALM 119:11 KJV

Europe in the early sixteenth century was ruled by the Catholic Church. Those who disagreed with its decisions were accused of heresy and sentenced to death.

William Tyndale was born in England in 1494, and he dreamed of translating the Bible into his native language—a task deemed heretical by the Catholic hierarchy. During a dinner with church officials at Little Sodbury Manor in Gloucestershire, Tyndale argued the importance of scripture. One church leader remarked that he would rather have the pope's laws than God's laws.

Enraged, Tyndale answered, "I defy the Pope and all his laws. . . . If God spare my life ere many years, I will cause the boy that driveth the plow to know more of the scriptures than thou dost."

William Tyndale believed God's Word should be available for everyone to read in their native language. . .and he was willing to die for that belief. Today, we can read from any number of English Bible translations—but do we? Is reading the Bible as important to you as it was to William Tyndale?

Lord, please make Your Word precious to me.
May I hide it in my heart so I don't sin against You.

PLUCKED FROM THE FIRE

And the LORD said to Satan, "I, the LORD, reject your accusations, Satan. Yes, the LORD, who has chosen Jerusalem, rebukes you. This man is like a burning stick that has been snatched from the fire."
ZECHARIAH 3:2 NLT

John Wesley was born in Epworth, England, in 1703 to Samuel and Susanna Wesley. John's father was the rector of Epworth.

By the end of his life, John Wesley was described as "the best loved man in England." In earning that title, he had traveled many miles preaching the gospel, laying a foundation on which the Methodist church would be built.

When John was five years old, he had an experience that he remembered for the rest of his life. One evening, while the Wesleys were asleep, the rectory roof caught fire. His siblings were all ushered from the home, but John was stranded on the second floor. As the house was about to collapse, John ran to a window where a Good Samaritan, standing on another man's shoulders, pulled the boy to safety.

God saved John Wesley from an earthly fire, just as Jesus Christ saves us from the fires of hell. Today, thank God for Jesus and the many ways He has kept you safe.

Father, thank You for saving my body from earthly dangers and my soul from the punishment for sin.

HOLY CLUB MEMBER

*But now you must be holy in everything you do,
just as God who chose you is holy. For the Scriptures
say, "You must be holy because I am holy."*
1 PETER 1:15–16 NLT

If you've ever been ridiculed for something, you know the emotional toll that can take. And when people give you or your friends a derogatory nickname, it can be even worse.

George Whitefield, born in 1714, put himself through Pembroke College at Oxford by waiting on the wealthier students as a servant of sorts. At Oxford, he met John and Charles Wesley whose influence led to Whitefield's new birth in Christ. The three of them met regularly to discuss classic literature, read the Bible, pray, and engage in Christian service. Soon, Whitefield and the Wesleys were derisively nicknamed the "Holy Club" by other students. They were dismissed as religious fanatics.

As you may already know, the Wesleys went on to start the Methodist church movement and Whitefield became the best-known itinerant preacher in America. He delivered more than eighteen thousand sermons in his thirty years of ministry.

If someone ever gives you a nickname, may it be for how much you love Jesus. Then wear that nickname proudly.

*Lord, may the derisive names people call me bring
glory to You—because of my love for You.*

FINDING A PURPOSE

*Defend the weak and the fatherless; uphold
the cause of the poor and the oppressed.*
PSALM 82:3 NIV

William Wilberforce, a member of the British Parliament, campaigned for the abolition of the slave trade, the rights of working-class citizens, universal access to education, and the prevention of cruelty to animals. With such a list of social reform issues, you might guess that he personally knew what it meant to be powerless.

But Wilberforce, born in 1759 in Hull, England, was the son of a wealthy merchant. When he turned twenty-one, he was elected to Parliament in part because of his social connections.

For a witty and eloquent speaker, this new position fit William perfectly. What his career did *not* do was provide meaning to his life. Looking back years later, he said, "The first years in Parliament I did nothing—nothing to any purpose. My own distinction was my darling object." It was not until he found Jesus Christ in his mid-twenties that William Wilberforce changed focus from himself to advocating for those without a voice.

Whether or not we hold official positions of leadership, most of us have some amount of influence. How can you use yours to help others less fortunate?

*Father, help me to use my power and
privilege for the benefit of others.*

MORNING STAR OF THE REFORMATION

> *"Those who are wise will shine as bright as the sky, and those who lead many to righteousness will shine like the stars forever."*
> DANIEL 12:3 NLT

Were it not for the groundbreaking work of many brave men, we might not have the Bible in any language other than Latin. John Wycliffe is one of those people—he helped translate God's Word into English and paved the way for such reformers as Jan Hus and Martin Luther. He's been called the "Morning Star of the Reformation."

John was born roughly two hundred miles from London around the year 1330. By 1346, he was studying at Oxford, during the era of the Black Death. He would earn his doctorate many years later, in 1372.

During his time at Oxford, in his study of God's Word, John Wycliffe realized that *Unam Sanctum*, which declared papal supremacy, had no root in scripture. At that point he began his quest to get scripture into the hands of everyone.

The Bible speaks into our hearts, our churches, and our culture. John Wycliffe became a forefather of the Reformation by delving deeply into God's Word. Follow his example and study your Bible. . .it will change your life.

Lord, provide clarity when I read scripture.
I will submit my life to its instruction.

CHRIST ABOVE ALL

Jesus replied, "No one who puts a hand to the plow and looks back is fit for service in the kingdom of God."
LUKE 9:62 NIV

The pursuit of Christ can take many roads. For Dietrich Bonhoeffer, the road was intellectual. He earned a college degree from the University of Berlin and, after a brief stint in Spain as an assistant pastor, returned to Germany to complete his dissertation. After that, Dietrich spent a year lecturing at the Union Theological Seminary in New York before returning to Germany.

As Bonhoeffer's education reached its pinnacle, another individual reached the height of his influence over the German people: Adolf Hitler.

It was then that Bonhoeffer, along with theologian Karl Barth and pastor Martin Niemoller, became outspoken opponents of Hitler and the Nazi party. As the German church succumbed to Nazi influence this trio started a movement called the Confessing Church, which publicly announced in 1934 that its primary allegiance was to Jesus Christ.

Can you imagine yourself in Bonhoeffer's situation? Similar pressures may be coming in the United States and other "Christian" societies. Ask God today to strengthen your faith and commitment to Jesus as Lord.

Father, there are many things that wish to be king of my life today. I want to place Christ first.

JOY, NOT DESPAIR

The LORD appeared to us in the past, saying:
"I have loved you with an everlasting love;
I have drawn you with unfailing kindness."
JEREMIAH 31:3 NIV

After World War II ended, the Netherlands sent Andrew van der Bijl overseas to fight in the Indonesian War of Independence. He was there to suppress the Indonesian people and keep them under Dutch rule. Andrew killed people in battle, was wounded himself, and turned to alcohol to soothe his internal turmoil.

While recuperating in the hospital, he was cared for by Franciscan nuns. Andrew was surprised by their joy and wondered where it came from. The nuns pointed to the Bible that had belonged to Andrew's mother—a keepsake he always carried with him. This ignited a curiosity for what was underneath the book's leather cover.

Not long after his experience—with the memory of those joyful nuns and some consistent exposure to the scriptures—Andrew van der Bijl dedicated his life to Jesus Christ.

When you are hurting and in need of encouragement, make Brother Andrew your example. Look to joyful Christian brothers and sisters—and the Bible they love—for encouragement.

Father, build up an overflowing joy within me that
I may draw others to your precious son, Jesus.

CHIEF AMONG SINNERS

For all have sinned, and come short of the glory of God.
ROMANS 3:23 KJV

Returning home from the English Civil War, John Bunyan got married and started attending church—but that didn't stop him from living frivolously. Then one day, a sermon about keeping the Sabbath day holy left him shaking.

Hours later, the guilt passed. . .and John returned to his vices. While playing a game with friends, though, he heard a voice say, "Wilt thou leave thy sins and go to heaven, or have thy sins and go to hell?"

Twice convicted in a day! One would hope that Bunyan experienced an immediate change. He didn't. In fact, he figured since he was already bound for hell, he should live as sinfully as possible.

Have you ever been convicted by something you heard in church or read in the Bible, then immediately returned to your old behavior? Do you ever justify sin with the thought that you'll be forgiven later? Those are shallow and dangerous ways of thinking. John Bunyan eventually discovered God's "grace abounding" that broke his desire for the things of the world. Ask the Lord to show you that grace, as well.

Lord, forgive me for using Your forgiveness
as an excuse to keep sinning. Break me
of my sin and help me live for You.

ANSWERING THE CALL

> *Above all, love each other deeply, because*
> *love covers over a multitude of sins.*
> 1 PETER 4:8 NIV

As John Calvin developed his mind, showing aptitude in many academic subjects, his father asked him to focus on law. John's heart was bent toward theology, but out of respect for his father, he listened.

Although John didn't know it at the time, this change in direction would lead him directly back to what he'd left.

While studying law in Paris, he excelled in Latin, was exposed to Renaissance ideas, and found himself drawn to the teachings of Martin Luther. Soon he was marked as one of Luther's followers just as Lutherans came under persecution in Paris. John fled west to Basel, Switzerland.

In a foreign land, John's heart broke for French commoners, his countrymen, and he wondered how he might share his new understanding of Christ with them. He decided to write a book, *The Institutes of the Christian Religion*.

Sometimes we find ourselves in strange places, unable to do the things we want to do. But if we stay pliable in God's hands, He'll use us in His own ways—which we'll probably find very fulfilling.

> *Lord, wherever I am, give me a heart*
> *to serve the people around me.*

INTERNATIONAL ENTHUSIAST

*The people walking in darkness have seen
a great light; on those living in the land of
deep darkness a light has dawned.*
ISAIAH 9:2 NIV

As William Carey's faith grew, his heart was drawn to Jesus' Great Commission in Matthew 28:19 (NIV): "Therefore go and make disciples of all nations, baptizing them in the name of the Father and of the Son and of the Holy Spirit." Interested in international cultures, William zeroed in on that "all nations" phrase, which would shape his entire life.

Carey began preaching in the "Particular Baptist" church. In one meeting he brought up the topic of international missions to which a senior member retorted, "Young man, sit down! You are an enthusiast. When God pleases to convert the heathen, he'll do it without consulting you or me."

In spite of such opposition, William was undeterred. He continued to incorporate the idea of foreign missions into his sermons and sought support among the local faith community. In time, he would be known as the "father of modern missions."

William Carey combined his own passion with a command of scripture, and truly changed the world. What topics are you inherently drawn to? How can you use those passions to serve Jesus Christ?

---

*Father, fill me with passion for those people—
near and far—who do not know Christ.*

REJECTED AND ACCEPTED

"If the world hates you, remember that it hated me first."
JOHN 15:18 NLT

As a young man, George Washington Carver pursued education wherever he could. At age thirteen, he left home to attend a school for black children in Neosho, Missouri. He boarded there with a kind woman who gave him a Bible and a mission: "You must learn all you can, then go back out into the world and give your learning back to the people."

George moved often to seek work and educational opportunities. After applying to numerous colleges, he was accepted by Highland University in northeastern Kansas. But upon his arrival, school administrators saw his skin color and refused him entrance.

A few years later, George was admitted to Iowa State Agricultural College (now Iowa State University) as its first black student. He excelled in agriculture and botany.

God had a plan for George Washington Carver that one school's rejection could not thwart. If this world rejects you—for your race, your faith, or anything else—take comfort because it rejected Jesus too. It doesn't matter if all of creation rejects you when you've been accepted by God.

Lord Jesus, You know rejection better than anyone. Help me feel Your acceptance so the world's rejection is meaningless.

FROM SLAVERY TO FREEDOM

I waited patiently for the LORD;
he turned to me and heard my cry.
PSALM 40:1 NIV

After Frederick Douglass found Christ, his life changed course—but not as you might expect.

Born a slave, he was fortunate to serve as a boy in the home of a Baltimore woman who treated him respectfully. As a young teen, he was introduced to Jesus by free blacks. But then he was sent from the city to the countryside and assigned to work as a field hand.

Frederick witnessed and experienced bloody beatings at the hand of a "slavebreaker." Physically, emotionally, and spiritually distressed, he cried out, "O, why was I born a man, of whom to make a brute! . . . I am left in the hottest hell of unending slavery. O God, save me! God, deliver me! Let me be free! Is there any God? Why am I a slave?"

After three horrendous years, Frederick was sent back to Baltimore, where he escaped to freedom. He took little with him but his deep faith in Christ. . .and a desire to challenge injustice in the world.

Are you suffering injustice? Do you know people who are? Cry out to God. He hears and answers the prayers of His people.

Father, I feel there is nowhere to turn
but to You. Be my shield today.

HAPPINESS IN THE AGE OF ENLIGHTENMENT

*Take delight in the LORD, and he will give
you the desires of your heart.*
PSALM 37:4 NIV

The Age of Enlightenment, beginning with the work of Isaac Newton, ushered in a new era of scientific study and dependence on reason. While others in this "age of reason" found God unnecessary, Jonathan Edwards saw science and reason as further evidence of God's existence. As such, he believed that truly reasonable people could find happiness only in a relationship with God.

In 1733, Edwards preached, "God is the highest good of the reasonable creature, and the enjoyment of him is the only happiness with which our souls can be satisfied. To go to heaven fully to enjoy God, is infinitely better than the most pleasant accommodations here. Fathers and mothers, husbands, wives, children, or the company of earthly friends, are but shadows. But the enjoyment of God is the substance. These are but scattered beams, but God is the sun. These are but streams, but God is the fountain. These are but drops, but God is the ocean."

Are you enjoying God for who He is? Never settle for the shadowy pleasures this life provides.

---

*Lord, help me not mistake the blessings of this world
for the enjoyment of my relationship with You.*

SENSING THE CALL

> *He called you to this through our gospel, that you*
> *might share in the glory of our Lord Jesus Christ.*
> 2 THESSALONIANS 2:14 NIV

In the fall of 1945, Jim Elliot left Oregon for Illinois, to attend Wheaton College. He disciplined himself to focus only on his studies and God.

After his sophomore year, Jim spent a portion of his summer in Mexico. He felt deeply connected to the people, and it became clear that God was calling him to serve in missions.

Jim completed college and moved back to Oregon, but only briefly. In 1950 he attended the Summer Institute of Linguistics in Oklahoma to learn how to study unwritten languages. Jim met a missionary from Ecuador, who described the peoples who dwelt deep in the jungle. At that point, Jim began to pray about serving in Ecuador, and God told him to go.

Few of us will be sent to a dark Ecuadorian jungle, but we can have an impact for Christ right where we are. Who are the lost people in your life? How can you reach out to just one of them today?

Father, today I listen for Your call. Show me who needs
to hear from You and use me as Your messenger.

ON LONDON'S STREETS

*For I am not ashamed of the gospel, because it is
the power of God that brings salvation to everyone
who believes: first to the Jew, then to the Gentile.*
ROMANS 1:16 NIV

Years before he founded the Salvation Army, while working as a pawnbroker's apprentice in London, William Booth preached anywhere he could. In 1852, he left his job to enter full-time ministry. Around this time, he also met Catherine Mumford, a woman who shared his passion for evangelism. They were married in 1855.

Moving from parish to parish, the Booths burned with a desire to reach the lost. Unfortunately, William's role as a congregational preacher didn't leave him much time for evangelism, so he and Catherine headed back to London where they knew the need was great. "Go for souls," William said, "and go for the worst." In East London, among the gin shops and brothels, the Booths got to work.

Zeal for evangelism is one mark of a vibrant relationship with Jesus Christ. From personal evangelism to street preaching, William and Catherine shared God's love to those in the greatest need.

Are you on fire to share Jesus' love with the lost? If your zeal is weak, pray about it!

*Lord, light my fire. May I burn with
a passion for the gospel.*

Billy Graham

THE TARZAN YELL

*Behold, I will do a new thing; now it shall spring
forth; shall ye not know it? I will even make a way
in the wilderness, and rivers in the desert.*
ISAIAH 43:19 KJV

As a boy in the 1920s, when he wasn't busy with school or working on his family's dairy farm, Billy Graham enjoyed reading Edgar Rice Burroughs's Tarzan stories. The books describe a child raised by apes; when he entered the world of men, he sought to do what was right among them.

Tarzan so inspired Billy that the boy would often climb trees and give his version of the Tarzan yell, frightening horses and passersby. Later in life, Billy's father said, "I think that yelling helped develop his voice."

It's possible this childhood love of adventure novels helped prepare Billy Graham for his world-traveling ministry as an adult. Either way, Billy went on to tell millions of people about a Man raised in an alien world who sought not only to do right, but to make things right between sinners and God.

If you ever hear a Tarzan yell, think of it as a call of praise—and use your voice like Billy Graham did, to share the good news of Jesus.

*Lord, thank You for making things
right between Yourself and us.*

FIFTEEN YEARS OF WINTER

*Two are better than one, because they have a
good return for their labor: If either of them falls
down, one can help the other up. But pity anyone
who falls and has no one to help them up.*
ECCLESIASTES 4:9 10 NIV

C. S. Lewis' early years were shaped by the Church of Ireland and the piles of books in his home. But one circumstance above all changed the course of the ten-year-old boy's life: the death of his mother.

Lewis prayed fervently for her recovery from cancer, but when she succumbed to the disease, his faith crumbled. Another blow to his Christianity came months later when his father sent him to boarding school. In five years, C. S. Lewis would lay aside his Christian faith entirely; fifteen years passed before he returned, due in part to the influence of his friend J. R. R. Tolkien, author of *The Lord of the Rings*.

Personal losses and unanswered prayers can cause us all to question God's plan. But Jesus has said that we will face trials in this life (John 16:33). Christian brothers can help tremendously. Today, seek out a reliable friend in the faith—and be one.

*Father, I ask You to place faithful Christians in my
life and give me the desire for their company.*

FOR GOD OR KING?

Do you not know that in a race all the
runners run, but only one gets the prize?
Run in such a way as to get the prize.
1 CORINTHIANS 9:24 NIV

With a singular focus on running, Eric Liddell climbed to the pinnacle of the sport: the Olympic games. First, in 1921, '22, and '23, he competed in the Triangular International Contests, which showcased athletes from England, Ireland, and Scotland. Eric won the sprints, giving him a spot on the British Olympic team that would compete in Paris, France, in 1924.

Eric was slated to run a heat of his best event, the 100-meter race, but learned it was scheduled for a Sunday. Because he believed that was a sabbath day of rest, he withdrew, opting instead to run the 400 meters on another day. Liddell was familiar with the longer race, but not a favorite to win.

His decision provoked outrage among British fans, who went so far as to question why he was placing God above winning a medal for the king.

There will be times when every committed Christian life will conflict with society. How will you respond when the decision time comes?

Lord, thank You for granting me victory in
what I do. You are the reason I succeed.

THE LION ATTACK

> *Stay alert! Watch out for your great enemy,*
> *the devil. He prowls around like a roaring*
> *lion, looking for someone to devour.*
> 1 PETER 5:8 NLT

During his first mission to Africa, David Livingstone was stationed in Bechuanaland, modern-day Botswana. While there, he responded to a call from a nearby village overtaken by a troop of lions. Livingstone called for a lion hunt, figuring if at least one lion could be killed, the rest would leave the village alone.

During the action, Livingstone took a shot at a lion, but it didn't immediately kill the beast. It attacked, severely mauling Livingstone's arm before the injured animal was finally put down. Though the missionary recovered, he never regained his full range of motion and dealt with pain for the rest of his life.

Lions are dangerous—and the Bible uses them as a metaphor for Satan. Our enemy is always seeking opportunities to attack us, and if we're not prepared, we leave ourselves vulnerable to serious injury. How do we prepare? We read and study God's Word. Pray that His Spirit would open your eyes to both the dangers and the solutions.

Lord, protect me from Satan's attacks. Heal me
from the injuries I've already incurred by my sins.

THE TRUTH ABOUT FAITH

> *For therein is the righteousness of God revealed from faith to faith: as it is written, The just shall live by faith.*
> ROMANS 1:17 KJV

After leaving law school, Martin Luther sought to perfect his faith through monasticism. He fasted, prayed, confessed regularly, and flagellated himself in the hopes of drawing closer to Christ. His efforts were in vain.

But as he meditated on Romans 1:17, the truth of faith dawned on him. God's righteousness is not revealed to the already faithful, because no one is righteous in themselves. God's righteousness is revealed to those whom God makes righteous. Faith in God is possible because it is a gift from God given while we are yet undeserving. . .and it comes because of Christ's sacrifice on our behalf.

"When I discovered that, I was born again of the Holy Ghost," said Luther, "and the doors of paradise swung open, and I walked through."

Praise God that He makes it possible for us to have faith in Him, to claim His righteousness as our own, and to live wholly for Him by that faith. Luther's realization that faith alone is the prerequisite for salvation was about to change the Church. It can change you too.

Lord, thank You for sharing Your righteousness with me.

SUNDAY SCHOOL IN THE SLUMS

Train up a child in the way he should go:
and when he is old, he will not depart from it.
PROVERBS 22:6 KJV

In 1856, D. L. Moody went to Chicago to make his living selling shoes. He became involved at Plymouth Congregational Church but was repeatedly advised not to attempt public speaking.

Undaunted, Moody looked outside the church, settling on a depraved district in northern Chicago called "The Sands." Moody set up Sunday school and evening Bible classes in an abandoned saloon and gave maple sugar to attendees.

A visiting friend named Reynolds remembered, "I went there a little late and the first thing I saw was a man standing up with a few tallow candles around him, holding a negro boy, and trying to read to him the story of the Prodigal Son; and a great many words he could not read out, and had to skip."

After that meeting, Moody pulled Reynolds aside and said, "I have got only one talent; I have no education, but I love the Lord Jesus Christ, and I want to do something for him: I want you to pray for me."

Reynolds prayers were effective. Through prayer, God can make any meager effort effective for Him.

Lord, I love You. Use my efforts for Your glory.

THROUGH THE JUNGLE

*He found him in a desert land, and in the waste
howling wilderness; he led him about, he instructed
him, he kept him as the apple of his eye.*
DEUTERONOMY 32:10 KJV

The African prince Kaboo miraculously escaped the captivity of an enemy tribe and ran for the jungle. He traveled by night, hiding in the hollows of trees during the day, always heading west toward the ocean.

Kaboo reached Monrovia on the coast and found work on a coffee plantation. A boy from his tribe who also worked there invited Kaboo to church. Though he didn't understand the English spoken, Kaboo felt the peace and presence of God.

Shortly afterward, a missionary told Kaboo about the apostle Paul's encounter with a bright light and voice from heaven, and how he'd been saved from his life of anger and hatred. Kaboo recognized that God had freed him as well. Kaboo came to Christ—and just as Saul became Paul, he was renamed Samuel Morris, in honor of the missionary's benefactor.

Like Kaboo, God is bringing you through the wilderness to Himself. When you read the Bible, watch for the ways God has written your story into its pages. Allow it to change you as it did Paul and Samuel Morris.

*Lord, give me eyes to see myself in Your Word.
Bring me through the wilderness to Yourself.*

PERSISTENCE IN PRAYER

> *Pray without ceasing.*
> 1 THESSALONIANS 5:17 KJV

If you've attended a Bible-teaching church for any amount of time, you've probably heard this verse. It's short, powerful. . .and seemingly impossible. *Pray without ceasing?* Does that mean I have to pray 24-7, 365 days a year? When do I sleep? How can I watch the occasional football broadcast?

The apostle Paul wasn't calling for nonstop prayer—but he did want Christians to keep praying until their answer comes. That is, don't cease praying before God has granted your request.

When George Müller felt God's leading to build a large orphanage in the British countryside, he began to pray. And he prayed. And he prayed. At one point, he wrote in his journal, "It is now four hundred days since I have been waiting upon God for help to build the Orphan House." For some reason, God was delaying the actual construction, but Müller could look back and see that his prayers for land and money had been answered. "I am not waiting upon the Lord in vain!" he wrote. "By His help, I am resolved to continue this course to the end."

That's praying without ceasing.

Lord God, please strengthen my resolve to pray without ceasing—to pray until You give me an answer.

GLORIOUS LOCAL CHURCH

*Just as a body, though one, has many parts, but all
its many parts form one body, so it is with Christ.*
1 CORINTHIANS 12:12 NIV

Watchman Nee had his own approach to sharing the gospel. He didn't hold revival meetings as he'd heard was occurring in other parts of the world. God revealed to Watchman that it was through local churches that China would be reached.

Watchman wrote that God had impressed upon him that "before long He would raise up local churches in various parts of China." From that time on, "whenever I closed my eyes, the vision of the birth of local churches appeared."

To encourage the growth of local churches, Watchman Nee traveled widely. He didn't have a steady, paying job, and since the economic situation in 1920s China was dire, he rarely ate a full meal. Living on a few bites of bread a day left him often in ill health, and he even battled tuberculosis for several years.

But Watchman Nee dedicated himself entirely to God's work. Personal comfort was not a priority for him. Can we say the same thing? What might you give up this week to pursue the Lord more fully?

---

*Father, raise up Your church to serve. Not just one
mighty leader, but each person ready to pursue Christ.*

LOWER THAN SLAVES

*Pride goes before destruction,
a haughty spirit before a fall.*
PROVERBS 16:18 NIV

As a young man in 1743, John Newton was pressed into British naval service aboard the HMS *Harwich*. Appeals to his father led to Newton becoming a midshipman, but he was not excused from service as John had hoped. In time, he deserted, only to be caught, put in irons, and flogged.

Seeking freedom from the Royal Navy's rigid life, Newton took up with a slaver named Clow who had an island plantation off West Africa. Clow's wife, Princess Peye of the Sherbro people, took an immediate dislike to Newton. When he fell ill, she denied him treatment and food. When he complained to Clow about the injustice, he was treated worse. Even the slaves took pity on John and fed him when they could.

In 1748, Newton was rescued when his father commissioned a ship captain to search for him. The prodigal son had learned humility, but his journey was far from over. God allowed John Newton to hit rock bottom so he could look up to heaven for help. Wouldn't it be better to just humble ourselves sooner rather than later?

*Lord, I know my desires apart from You lead to slavery.
Free me from my sins and restore me as Your child.*

ON TRUE WEALTH

> *"Don't store up treasures here on earth, where moths
> eat them and rust destroys them, and where thieves
> break in and steal. Store your treasures in heaven,
> where moths and rust cannot destroy, and thieves
> do not break in and steal. Wherever your treasure
> is, there the desires of your heart will also be."*
> MATTHEW 6:19–21 NLT

Within years of his father's death when Luis Palau was only ten, the family was driven to poverty. Luis left boarding school and became a trainee at a bank in Córdoba, Argentina.

For many people, being poor and working around money might have awakened desires to seek wealth for themselves. But his mother's example of faith was a stronger influence, and Luis came to value Christian service even more.

"Basketball players and musicians are not my heroes; they're just gifted millionaires," he wrote in *Palau: A Life on Fire*. "Those who give their lives for the service of others, those who put their own comfort or safety aside to bring the Good News of Jesus to people who have never heard—they are the real heroes."

When this world passes away, all its physical wealth pass away too. Only those who store their treasures in heaven will have something to offer God.

*Lord, please keep my priorities straight
when I'm tempted to idolize wealth.*

PUT ON CHRIST

> *Immediately, something like scales fell from Saul's eyes,*
> *and he could see again. He got up and was baptized.*
> ACTS 9:18 NIV

In AD 386, when he was thirty-two years old, Augustine was with a friend in Milan when he heard children singing, "Pick it up and read it, pick it up and read it." He thought the words were part of a game but soon concluded that God was speaking to him about scripture.

So Augustine obeyed. He first read Romans 13:13–14 (NIV), which says, "Let us behave decently, as in the daytime, not in carousing and drunkenness, not in sexual immorality and debauchery, not in dissension and jealousy. Rather, clothe yourselves with the Lord Jesus Christ, and do not think about how to gratify the desires of the flesh."

The passage brought conviction to Augustine's soul, but also the light that can only come from salvation. He turned completely from his sin and was baptized by Saint Ambrose.

We will read many things in scripture that convict us—and that's a good thing. But it's an even better thing if we respond as Augustine did, by turning from our sin.

Lord, please search my life and show me
what I have yet to give fully to You.

FIRST IMPRESSIONS

"Look beneath the surface so you can judge correctly."
JOHN 7:24 NLT

Four years after his conversion, Charles Spurgeon was invited to preach at New Park Street Chapel, the largest Baptist congregation in London.

One woman who attended the session recalled, "I was not at all fascinated by the young orator's eloquence, while his countrified manner and speech excited more regret than reverence. Alas, for my vain and foolish heart! I was not spiritually-minded enough to understand his earnest presentation of the gospel, and his powerful pleading with sinners—but the huge black satin stock, the long badly-trimmed hair, and the blue pocket-handkerchief with white spots—these attracted most of my attention, and, I fear, awakened some feelings of amusement."

In spite of this woman's first impressions, Charles was called to become the church's pastor—and she went on to become his wife.

Do new experiences frighten you? If God has something in mind for you, it will happen. If He hasn't ordained something to be, it won't. Your job is to simply do your best with what you have. Trust Him to take care of the details.

Lord, help me trust Your plan for me.
Keep me doing the next right thing for You.

TRANSFORMATION

*Put on your new nature, and be renewed as you
learn to know your Creator and become like him.*
COLOSSIANS 3:10 NLT

When major league baseball player Billy Sunday gave his life to Christ, his teammates noticed a drastic change in his behavior. Before his conversion, Billy would visit bars with the other players; now he avoided drinking altogether. He denounced swearing and gambling and pursued his new life with such conviction that even fans took notice.

Billy played professionally from 1883 until 1890. The next year, he was offered a contract for thirty-five hundred dollars, but declined it to take a job at the YMCA, where he earned eighty-three dollars a month. This new position gave Billy a chance to care for the sick and suicidal, and to pray for people who requested it. He even went back to the bars—to invite people to meetings.

Along with his conversion, Billy Sunday felt a call to preach. Lacking theological training, he aimed for the masses. "I want to preach the gospel so plainly," he said, "that men can come from the factories and not have to bring a dictionary." Soon he became a traveling evangelist.

When he decided to follow Jesus, Billy Sunday's priorities changed completely. Can we say the same of our lives today?

Father, help me to pursue You with all my heart.

ADAPTABLE FAITH

> *When I was with the Jews, I lived like a Jew to bring
> the Jews to Christ. When I was with those who follow
> the Jewish law, I too lived under that law. Even
> though I am not subject to the law, I did this so I
> could bring to Christ those who are under the law.*
> 1 CORINTHIANS 9:20 NLT

In 1851, preparing for missionary service in China, Hudson Taylor moved to a poorer part of London to work as a medical assistant. While there, trusting God to provide for his needs, he heard about the new Chinese Evangelisation Society. Hudson volunteered as the organization's first missionary.

Two years later, he left for China. Upon his arrival, though, Hudson discovered a significant barrier to sharing his faith: the Chinese referred to him as a "black devil" because of the coat he wore. He responded by shaving his forehead, growing a queue (a long pigtail), and swapping his coat for traditional Chinese clothing. This helped his evangelism, though it drew the ire of fellow missionaries.

Truly following Jesus may mean bucking tradition—even the trends of our current Christian circles. But obedience to the Lord supersedes everything else—as the apostle Peter once said, "We must obey God rather than any human authority" (Acts 5:29 NLT).

> *Lord, help me honor You in everything—including
> my adaptability in sharing the gospel.*

THE KING'S LOOPHOLE

Christ is also the head of the church, which is his body. He is the beginning, supreme over all who rise from the dead. So he is first in everything.
COLOSSIANS 1:18 NLT

Few writers can claim to have changed the course of history with a book, but William Tyndale could make the claim. In 1528, he published *The Obedience of a Christian Man*, which argued the king of a country—rather than the pope—should be head of that country's church.

Tyndale's book heavily influenced Henry VIII's 1534 decision to declare himself the head of the church in England. The move was in response to the pope's refusal to allow Henry to annul his marriage to Catherine of Aragon. Tyndale opposed the king's divorce too, but his book had provided the king with the loophole he sought.

Of course, no earthly king is head of Christ's church—Jesus Himself is. And in His divine justice, there are no loopholes. He is the only way to heaven, the only remedy for sin on earth. We make a serious mistake by pretending to be king of our own lives. If that's your case, abdicate today. Make room for the King of kings.

Lord, keep me off Your throne.
You are the true king of my life.

FAITH, NOT KNOWLEDGE

> *"You can identify them by their fruit, that
> is, by the way they act. Can you pick grapes
> from thornbushes, or figs from thistles?"*
> MATTHEW 7:16 NLT

John Wesley attended Oxford, graduating at the age of twenty-one. Afterward, he was ordained a deacon, completed his Master's degree, and served as priest in a church near his hometown.

All of this prepared him for ministry to British colonists in the New World. While voyaging to Savannah, Georgia, in 1735–36, the ship encountered a fierce storm. Wesley was terrified. Others on board were not.

He noticed that a group of German Moravians, on their way to preach to American Indians, showed no fear at all. In fact, throughout the storm, they calmly sang and prayed. When the trip ended, Wesley asked the Moravian leader about his serenity. The response was a question: Did Wesley have faith in Christ? He said he did, but later reflected, "I fear they were vain words." Like many people, John Wesley knew who God was. But when troubles came, he realized his faith was lacking.

Never be satisfied with a head knowledge of God. . .ask the Lord to give you complete faith and trust in Him.

---

*Father, instead of an intellectual understanding,
fill me with steadfast faith in You.*

OUTDOOR PREACHER

> *"I tell you, whoever publicly acknowledges
> me before others, the Son of Man will also
> acknowledge before the angels of God."*
> LUKE 12:8 NIV

Upon graduating from college, George Whitefield was ordained in the Church of England and began preaching around London. His sermons reflected his childhood love of acting and were wholly unlike the preaching most Anglicans expected. Whitefield dramatized biblical scenes, moved energetically, cried, and even shouted from the pulpit.

Churches that previously hosted Whitefield began closing their doors to his dramatic sermons. So, without a building to preach in, Whitefield moved outdoors—and crowds showed up. Within a week, ten thousand people had come to hear him. Within a few months, crowds as large as fifty thousand heard him give the gospel message.

Whitefield didn't let closed doors stop him from preaching, and neither should we. The excuses that often keep us from sharing the gospel are simply that—excuses. Ask God for courage, then tell someone what the Lord has done for you. . .even if you have to take it outdoors!

---

*Lord, give me courage to share the gospel wherever
I am as boldly as George Whitefield did.*

PROPONENT OF THE POWERLESS

"This is what the LORD says: Do what is just and right. Rescue from the hand of the oppressor the one who has been robbed. Do no wrong or violence to the foreigner, the fatherless or the widow, and do not shed innocent blood in this place."
JEREMIAH 22:3 NIV

When William Wilberforce experienced the "Great Change" to follow Jesus, his focus shifted completely. He sold his racehorse, stopped gambling and drinking, and avoided dinner parties, saying they "disqualify me for every useful purpose in life, waste my time, impair my health, fill my mind with thoughts of resistance before and self-condemnation afterwards."

A friend introduced Wilberforce to the issue that would shape most of his life, the slave trade. Convinced that this was his purpose, William wrote, "So enormous, so dreadful, so irremediable did the trade's wickedness appear that my own mind was completely made up for abolition. Let the consequences be what they would: I from this time determined that I would never rest until I had effected its abolition."

Different people have different callings, but God has a job for each of His children. What issue grips your heart? What can you do today to effect a positive change?

Father, show me those in my life who are powerless and have no voice. Help me to act and speak for them.

THE ULTIMATE AUTHORITY

*All Scripture is inspired by God and is useful to
teach us what is true and to make us realize what
is wrong in our lives. It corrects us when we are
wrong and teaches us to do what is right.*
2 TIMOTHY 3:16 NLT

After his studies at Oxford, John Wycliffe became part of the faculty. He taught philosophy but was drawn to scripture. As he studied the Bible, he realized the church was far off course from what God's Word taught.

In the 1300s, the Catholic church was a formidable institution. But Wycliffe was a man of conviction. Between 1374 and 1378, he wrote three books that countered the church's teaching. The first, *On Divine Dominion*, argued that scripture, not the papacy, is the true authority for life. Next, *On Civil Dominion* challenged what Wycliffe saw as a corrupt Rome's authority over England. Finally, *On the Truth of Sacred Scripture* reinforced his views on the Bible as the true authority over people's lives. These books were foundational to the Reformation.

John Wycliffe used his talents to advance God's kingdom. Have you ever considered how your abilities might benefit the spread of the gospel? Take a moment today to ask God how He might use you as he did John Wycliffe.

---

*Father, show me how I may use my
talents to advance Your purposes.*

FULLY COMMITTED

*"Have I not commanded you? Be strong and courageous.
Do not be afraid; do not be discouraged, for the
LORD your God will be with you wherever you go."*
JOSHUA 1:9 NIV

As Germany succumbed to the allure of Nazi teachings, Dietrich Bonhoeffer helped establish the Confessing Church. This provided him with a platform to speak out against Adolf Hitler and his Nazi party. Bonhoeffer preached boldly that Christ should be the center of life.

This venture was short lived, though, as the church came under persecution and Bonhoeffer was forbidden to teach. This did not dissuade him, and he discovered and then taught at an underground seminary called Finkenwalde. No matter what his government said, Bonhoeffer would spread the gospel of Christ.

He was living out the apostle Paul's words to his protégé, Timothy: "The Spirit of God gave us does not make us timid, but gives us power, love and self-discipline" (2 Timothy 1:7 NIV).

When we face opposition to sharing our faith, it might seem reasonable to quietly retreat. But remember Dietrich Bonhoeffer: instead of giving up, he found other ways of sharing the love of Christ.

---

*Father, no matter the opposition or cost, may I
always make Christ the centerpiece of all that I do.*

ANSWERING THE CALL

*"For whoever wants to save their life will lose it,
but whoever loses their life for me will save it."*
LUKE 9:24 NIV

When Brother Andrew gave his life to Christ, he was unsure of his next step. After the Dutch lost the Indonesian War of Independence, he returned to his hometown in the Netherlands. It was there Andrew attended a missionary meeting and answered the call to share the joy and hope of salvation in Jesus.

From that point on, Andrew did not wait for a clear direction. He simply looked for opportunities to share his faith each day, right where he was.

He started a Bible study at the factory where he worked and became an encouragement to people around him. He attended the Glasgow Bible College in Scotland. He received a miraculous healing of the ankle that was injured while he fought in Indonesia. And he just kept serving God, one step at a time, with incredible results.

God will provide for His people who wish to share the gospel. And He's happy for you to start small. How can you share the good news of Jesus today, right where you are?

---

*Father, I look for Your direction in all I do. Help me
to live by faith and share it, right where I am.*

NEW BIRTH IN CHRIST

*Jesus answered and said unto him, Verily,
verily, I say unto thee, Except a man be born
again, he cannot see the kingdom of God.*
JOHN 3:3 KJV

After realizing his sinful state, John Bunyan tried to overcome his sins by sheer effort. He stopped swearing, put off friends of bad influence, and curbed his dancing habits. As his lifestyle changed, Bunyan felt sure that God was pleased.

Then one day, he overheard some women discussing religious matters. They spoke of their trials and temptations, of the new birth they had in Christ, and how their efforts to be righteous were insufficient to do them good. As he realized the truth of their words, Bunyan began to shake.

"I saw that in all my thoughts about religion and salvation, the new birth did never enter into my mind," he recalled, "neither knew I the comfort of the word and promise, nor the deceitfulness and treachery of my own wicked heart."

New birth in Christ makes all the difference. No matter how much we try to change for God, it will never be enough. As John Bunyan learned, God's love works from the inside out.

---

*Lord, thank You for salvation. Help me to act in Your love
instead of trying to earn Your love with my actions.*

ACCESS FOR ALL FRENCHMEN

> *For we are God's handiwork, created in Christ Jesus to do good works, which God prepared in advance for us to do.*
> EPHESIANS 2:10 NIV

When John Calvin fled Catholic persecution in Paris, he could not stop thinking of the countrymen he left behind. From his new base in Basel, Switzerland, he wondered how he might share Christ with them. The printing press was a new invention and the Bible had just been translated into French.

Calvin's solution was to write the *Institutes of the Christian Religion*. This would explain the pillars of Protestant belief. Most of the populace relied on pastors and priests for biblical interpretation. John's book aimed to bridge that gap.

"I labored at the task especially for our own Frenchmen," he said, "for I saw that many were hungering and thirsting after Christ and yet that only a very few had any real knowledge of him."

In his time and circumstances, John Calvin almost had to write a book. But that's not essential for us. In fact, it's quickest and easiest simply to talk with people!

> *Father, wherever I am, help me to use the gifts and desires You have placed in my heart to advance Your kingdom.*

GREAT THINGS

For the Spirit God gave us does not make us timid,
but gives us power, love and self-discipline.
2 TIMOTHY 1:7 NIV

William Carey belonged to an association of Particular Baptists. Although he was derided as a "miserable enthusiast," he rallied the group to form the Baptist Missionary Society. Carey charged them to "expect great things, attempt great things."

The men of the Baptist Missionary Society were of the same socioeconomic background as William—that is to say, poor. They raised a sum of money which today would be in the neighborhood of twenty-three dollars.

You might think this meager amount would deter William Carey. It was not enough to support even one missionary let alone two. But he volunteered, along with one of his best friends, to go to India.

Carey's desire to obey God's call looked precarious, especially considering that he was taking a wife and son to the field. The missionaries would face many hardships, from finances to health to the opposition of local authorities.

Have you ever felt a calling to serve but found opposition everywhere? Don't give up! Seek Christ. As He did with William Carey, He will sustain you and show the way.

Father, when seemingly insurmountable obstacles
appear in my path, may I trust You to guide me.

UNLOCKING THE GOLDEN DOOR

Intelligent people are always ready to learn.
Their ears are open for knowledge.
PROVERBS 18:15 NLT

Shortly after George Washington Carver completed his master of science degree, he was given the chance to head up a new agricultural program at the Tuskegee Institute in Alabama.

George accepted, saying, "it has always been the one great ideal of my life to be of the greatest good to the greatest number of 'my people' possible and to this end I have been preparing myself these many years; feeling as I do that this line of education is the key to unlock the golden door of freedom to our people."

As a former slave, George knew the doors an education could open. Over his lifetime, he had worked hard on farms, started a laundry business, speculated in real estate, and served as a hotel cook. . .but nothing had opened doors for him like education. Still, George knew it was God who had directed his path into learning. He prayed regularly that God would open his eyes to the wondrous things in His world. God was faithful to George's request, as He is to all who seek His truth.

Lord, make me ready and eager to learn.
Open my eyes to Your truth.

ABOLITIONIST LEADER

*"I am the LORD your God, who brought you
out of Egypt, out of the land of slavery."*
DEUTERONOMY 5:6 NIV

After escaping slavery, Frederick Douglass obtained an education,
married, and eventually settled in New Bedford, Massachusetts.
In 1841, at the age of twenty-three, he received an invitation that
would change his life: Frederick was asked to speak at an anti-
slavery convention in Nantucket, describing his life as a slave and
what he thought about slavery. He spoke so vividly and with such
eloquence that he was invited to become a prominent member
of the Massachusetts Anti-Slavery Society.

Frederick Douglass' career as a traveling speaker had barely
begun when hardships arose to meet him. He was insulted and
mocked. Onlookers heckled him from the crowd and attempts on
his life followed. Critics even turned his gift of speaking against
him, questioning whether he could have been a slave at all.

But he persevered, using his experience and eloquence against
injustice in the world. What good might you accomplish if you just
stay the course today?

---

*Father, when I face opposition to Your work,
fill me with boldness and endurance.*

SINNERS IN THE HANDS OF AN ANGRY GOD

And my message and my preaching were very plain.
Rather than using clever and persuasive speeches,
I relied only on the power of the Holy Spirit.
1 CORINTHIANS 2:4 NLT

Broadly recognized as one of America's greatest theologians, Jonathan Edwards is most famous for his sermon, "Sinners in the Hands of an Angry God." It was delivered at the height of the First Great Awakening in colonial America.

With its vivid images of hellfire and brimstone, you might assume Edwards preached the sermon in a dramatic way. In truth, he was a soft-spoken man, moving from point to point in a methodical—perhaps even boring—style. When congregants wept and shouted, frequently interrupting his sermon, it was not due to one man's abilities as a speaker, but by the influence of the Holy Spirit working through his sermon.

You don't have to be a polished speaker to point others to Jesus. Jonathan Edwards wasn't. Whenever the opportunity arises to share Christ—whether in a public or private setting—remember that it is the Holy Spirit who works through your words. The only personal ability you need is a willingness to speak.

Lord, may I use the gifts You have given to me in the power of the Holy Spirit to bring people to Your love.

OVERCOMING OBSTACLES

> *Therefore, my brothers and sisters, make every*
> *effort to confirm your calling and election. For if*
> *you do these things, you will never stumble.*
> 2 PETER 1:10 NIV

After college, Jim Elliot was not done learning. He continued his preparation for the mission field by studying the Bible vigorously and attending the Summer Institute of Linguistics to learn about unwritten languages. While there, Jim met a missionary retiring from Ecuador, the country Jim felt drawn to serve. He had both the heart and head knowledge. . .now he had an opportunity.

When Jim reached Quito, Ecuador, he faced new challenges. The people he desired to introduce to Jesus, the Waodani, were aggressive. Their villages were so remote that there was no landing strip nearby. And Jim and his missionary partner Pete Fleming could not speak Spanish.

But the duo learned Spanish in six months and the Lord provided help in approaching the tribe: a woman who had deserted the Waodani was willing to teach them the language and guide them to the community.

Jim Elliot "made every effort," to use the apostle Peter's phrase, to reach his goal. And because Jim Elliot worked, God did too. When He calls, He also provides. Our job is simply to stay faithful, no matter the obstacles.

> *Father, thank You for always providing*
> *a way forward when I work.*

DEVIL'S MUSIC AND WORLDLY CONVERTS

To the weak became I as weak, that I might
gain the weak: I am made all things to all men,
that I might by all means save some.
1 CORINTHIANS 9:22 KJV

As an evangelist, William Booth used uncommon methods to spread the gospel. When some Christians criticized his use of secular music to draw crowds, Booth would reply, "Secular music, do you say, belongs to the devil? Does it? Well, if it did I would plunder him for it, for he has no right to a single note of the whole seven."

In addition to music, William and Catherine Booth offered lively sermons and soup kitchens, feeding both the spirit and the soul.

Perseverance led to results. Thieves, prostitutes, and drunks were some of the Booths' earliest London converts, and these people sang praise to God and spread the word to others in need of salvation. Soon, an army of believers arose.

If you're discouraged when your efforts to spread the gospel are ineffective or met with derision, don't quit. Adjust your ways. A soul won for God through uncommon methods is still a soul won for God.

Lord, You came to save the lost.
Help me reach them however I can.

PASTOR BILLY'S RADIO SHOW

*For Christ did not send me to baptize, but to preach
the gospel—not with wisdom and eloquence, lest
the cross of Christ be emptied of its power.*
1 CORINTHIANS 1:17 NIV

After graduating from Wheaton Bible College outside Chicago, Billy Graham took on a brief pastoral ministry nearby. Although he served the Village Church of Western Springs for less than two years, Billy's time in church leadership set the course for much larger ministries later on.

Shortly after becoming pastor, Billy's friend Torrey Johnson said that his radio program was about to be canceled due to lack of funding. After much prayer, the Village Church took on the ministry's funding and programming with Billy Graham at the helm. Before long, that midwestern radio ministry (called *Songs in the Night*) was receiving hundreds of letters of support. But God had even bigger plans for Billy Graham.

He was a gifted communicator who would speak to millions, around the world, for decades. But you don't need to be eloquent for God to bless your words. After all, His power is most evident when we feel least able to do things on our own.

*Lord, make me faithful in sharing the
gospel to whomever needs to hear it.*

RELUCTANT CONVERT

"And everyone who calls on the name
of the Lord will be saved."
ACTS 2:21 NIV

When C. S. Lewis declared himself an atheist at age fifteen, he believed he was on a logical path of thought. He surmised that if there were cruelty and wrongdoing in the world, there must be no good and just God behind everything. His atheistic beliefs were reinforced when he experienced the horrors of World War I. Lewis himself was injured, and his good friend, Paddy Moore, killed.

When he recovered from his injuries, Lewis went to live with Paddy's mother and sister. He became a fellow of Magdalen College, Oxford, where he developed a friendship with several Christians, including J. R. R. Tolkien. One night, after a long conversation with Tolkien and another friend, Lewis realized the only reason he recognized injustice and evil is because something must be ultimately just and good—namely, God. He later wrote, "I gave in, and admitted that God was God. . .perhaps, that night, the most dejected and reluctant convert in all of England."

At times, we'll all wrestle with questions about the faith. But we don't have to do that alone. When things get confusing, seek out a pastor or respected Christian friend to guide your journey.

Father, thank You for wise Christians in my
life, people who help sharpen my faith.

THE SECRET OF SUCCESS

> *"Blessed is the one who trusts in the*
> *LORD, whose confidence is in him."*
> JEREMIAH 17:7 NIV

How many of your country's Olympic gold medalists can you name? Probably a few. But what if the question is narrowed down to the 1920s? Then the answer is "probably not many."

Would you be surprised to learn that, in a 2002 poll, Eric Liddell was nominated as the most popular Scottish sports figure of all time? His fame has lasted for nearly a century. Perhaps that has something to do with his humility.

After his victory, Eric shared how he was able to run so well in a race he had not trained for: "The secret of my success over the 400 meters is that I run the first 200 meters as fast as I can. Then, for the second 200 meters, with God's help I run faster."

Many would have understood if Eric Liddell claimed glory for himself. After all, he was an Olympic champion! But he chose to point toward the true source of his skill, the one who had made him.

The next time someone compliments your achievements or abilities, say, "thank you"—but then point them to the God who made your success possible.

> *Lord, thank You for granting me victories.*
> *You are the reason I succeed.*

MISSIONARY TO ONE

So neither the one who plants nor the one who waters
is anything, but only God, who makes things grow.
1 CORINTHIANS 3:7 NIV

Though famous for his mission work, David Livingstone is credited with reaching only one African during his time in ministry. Sechele, his single convert, was chief of the Bakwena tribe in what is now Botswana.

Missionaries were often welcome because they brought firearms and medicine with them, but Sechele was more interested in literacy. Livingstone taught him English and introduced him to the Bible. The chief was an eager convert, but within months went back to his polygamist ways. Livingstone soon moved on.

"Africa's greatest missionary" may have considered himself a failure, but God grew the seed David Livingstone had planted. Though Sechele never quit some aspects of his African beliefs, he translated the Bible into his language and converted his tribe to Christianity. His Bakwena people became ten times as populous as when Livingstone was with them, and Sechele even reached out to other tribes.

We won't always see the fruit of the gospel seeds we plant. But we can be sure that God will grow them in His time and His own way.

Lord, help me plant Your seed without expectation.
You are in charge of the increase.

Martin Luther

THE NINETY-FIVE THESES

If we confess our sins, he is faithful and just to forgive us our sins, and to cleanse us from all unrighteousness.
1 JOHN 1:9 KJV

As a professor of theology at the University of Wittenberg, Martin Luther didn't set out to start the Reformation. But his publication of the *Ninety-Five Theses* did just that.

Luther was raising a complaint with the Catholic church's sale of indulgences—certificates believed to reduce one's experience of punishment for sins. In his view, this practice led people into a false form of repentance. Why truly repent when you can buy indulgences and continue in your sins?

Before long, Luther's arguments spread across the Christian world, igniting the Reformation. . .and bringing true repentance with it.

Forgiveness of sins doesn't require a donation. God tells us that if we confess our sins, He will forgive us. Jesus has already paid our debt.

Once we are forgiven, we will want to give money back to God as an act of worship. But don't ever think anything we do is a means of forgiveness. Don't diminish the incredible work God has done on your behalf.

Lord, I need the forgiveness only You can give. I know I cannot pay for it, because You give it freely.

THE GREAT FIRE

*These have come so that the proven genuineness of
your faith—of greater worth than gold, which perishes
even though refined by fire—may result in praise,
glory and honor when Jesus Christ is revealed.*
1 PETER 1:7 NIV

Beginning October 8, 1871, the Great Chicago Fire killed three hundred people and left some ninety thousand people—about one in three residents—homeless. D. L. Moody quickly pitched in to help others, emerging days later, as he said, with "nothing but his reputation and his Bible."

Moody's church building was destroyed, and in succeeding months he raised funds for rebuilding. On the Sunday after its completion, a thousand children attended the service. The building was used for both church and community purposes.

But as his life and ministry were restored, D. L. Moody wrestled with a question: Was his previous ministry achievement based on a pursuit of God's glory or his own personal ambition? God used the fire to burn away Moody's ideas of success and ignite a passion for global evangelism in its place.

Ambition isn't all bad—it allows us to achieve bigger and better things. But if our own ambition gets in the way of God's best things, He may need to refine us "by fire."

*Lord, burn away the things that won't last,
and rebuild me to be the man You desire.*

SAILING TO AMERICA

> *"I tell you, you can pray for anything, and if you*
> *believe that you've received it, it will be yours."*
> MARK 11:24 NLT

Samuel Morris learned English working on a coffee plantation. After that, the former African prince painted houses for a living. . .but his real passion was to return to the Kru tribe as a preacher. When a missionary gave him advice, Samuel prayed about it.

"Father," he said, "you have called me to preach to my people, but the missionary says I can't preach without an education, and that to be educated I must go to America; and, Father, you know I have not a single cent—please make a way for me to go."

Having put the matter in God's hands, Samuel went to the docks and waited for a ship. Before long, he found one bound for New York, with a captain willing to hire him in exchange for his passage.

A few days into the voyage, Samuel became violently ill. But again he prayed that God would make a way. And soon he felt better.

Prayer is more than just talking with God. It is putting faith in your Father, believing that He will do what needs to be done. Are your prayers vague and generic, or specific and deep?

Father, grant me faith to believe You'll
help me get things done.

ALL THINGS ARE POSSIBLE

Jesus said unto him, If thou canst believe,
all things are possible to him that believeth.
MARK 9:23 KJV

Jesus spoke these words to the desperate father of a demon-possessed boy. Nineteen centuries later, George Müller applied them to his ministry to orphans.

In fact, this verse is one of several inscribed on a memorial stone at his grave. Erected by several of the children he served, it beautifully encapsulates Müller's brave reliance on God's Word and power: "He trusted in God with whom 'nothing shall be impossible,' and in His beloved Son Jesus Christ our Lord who said 'I go unto my Father, and whatsoever ye shall ask in my name that will I do that the Father may be glorified in the Son,' and in His inspired word which declares that 'all things are possible to him that believeth.' And God fulfilled these declarations in the experience of His servant by enabling him to provide and care for about ten thousand orphans."

What could God do through your own believing trust in Him?

Father in heaven, I want to believe in Your Word and
power like George Müller did. I want to accomplish
great things in people's lives for Your honor and glory.

FELLOWSHIP IN THE GOSPEL

*That is, that you and I may be mutually
encouraged by each other's faith.*
ROMANS 1:12 NIV

Watchman Nee was not alone in serving the Lord. Though he faced many obstacles, he had a nourishing fellowship with his fellow Christians, including one in particular: Witness Lee. Witness greatly admired Watchman, who was two years older. Their connection started via correspondence.

Watchman proved to be the encouragement that Witness needed to start a church in his own home. After Witness' house church began to thrive, Watchmen encouraged Witness to join him in Shanghai. While there, Witness helped edit Watchman's publication *The Christian* for half a decade. When Watchman was married, Witness was best man.

Good Christian friends can be hard to find. If you have a mentor or close Christian brother, make sure to thank them for encouraging your faith. And if you don't have one, go looking— you need that input. "As iron sharpens iron," Proverbs 27:17 (NIV) says, "so one person sharpens another."

*Father, thank You for the Christian brothers and
sisters in my life who encourage me. Please
provide a special blessing for them today.*

THROUGH THE STORM

> *But the LORD hurled a powerful wind*
> *over the sea, causing a violent storm that*
> *threatened to break the ship apart.*
> JONAH 1:4 NLT

After his rescue from Africa, John Newton's voyage back to England almost killed him.

After picking up Newton from a slaver's plantation, the ship he was on encountered problems. The captain joked they had a "Jonah" aboard, but the jest grew less funny as the trip wore on. When an intense storm struck in mid-Atlantic, the ship almost sank but for the fact that its cargo floated.

"When I saw, beyond all probability, there was still hope of respite," Newton recalled, "there arose a gleam of hope. I thought I saw the hand of God displayed in our favour: I began to pray."

It was the first prayer in a long while for a self-described "wretch," and it marked a turning point in his life. Four weeks later, the ship limped into harbor.

We'll all face storms in our lives, some of them strong enough to sink the "ships" of our homes, our finances, and our overall well-being. Like John Newton, we can only appeal to the God who controls the storm. Christians are always in His hands, even if the ship breaks up around them.

> *Lord, help me trust You. Bring me*
> *through the storm to Your safety.*

IMITATING BILLY GRAHAM VS. IMITATING GOD

*Imitate God, therefore, in everything you
do, because you are his dear children.*
EPHESIANS 5:1 NLT

In 1952, Luis Palau first heard Billy Graham preach on the radio. The young Argentinian prayed that God would help him become an evangelist like the famed American. Ten years later, Luis became a Spanish interpreter for Graham. But before that, he began his formal ministry as a preacher. There were missteps.

"I was in a little country church in the hills of Argentina," Palau recalled to an interviewer from *Christianity Today*. "There were probably thirty-five people in the little joint, and I thought, 'Oh, Billy Graham.' I had watched him in a film, and he shouted his head off in those days, and he waved his arms and paced back and forth. I thought I'd do the same. I made a fool of myself. Thirty-five people and I'm shouting like [I'm in] a stadium without microphones."

Luis Palau learned that imitating people is a tricky business. But it's always right to imitate God. When you live a life filled with love, you are truly reflecting the one who created, redeems, and keeps you—showing that you are His child.

*Lord, may people see me acting like You and
be inspired to love You because of it.*

HEARTS MADE FOR GOD

*You were taught, with regard to your former way of
life, to put off your old self, which is being corrupted
by its deceitful desires; to be made new in the attitude
of your minds; and to put on the new self, created
to be like God in true righteousness and holiness.*
EPHESIANS 4:22–24 NIV

Reflecting on his conversion experience years later, Augustine penned the famous prayer, "You have made us for yourself, Lord, and our hearts are restless until they rest in you." Augustine knew restlessness, as he had tried to find meaning everywhere. But he was unfulfilled until he gave his entire life to Christ.

From that time forward, Augustine made purposeful efforts to lay down anything in his life that was not aligned with Jesus. He sent away his concubine, his partner of fourteen years. He resigned from his post as a teacher of rhetoric and retreated to the country. Eighteen months after his conversion, he was baptized.

To follow Christ means to leave some of our former life behind. That's often difficult, but the first step is admitting that our old ways are corrupt and deceitful. Ask God to renew your mind and make you like Him.

*Father, show me what I need to remove from my own
life. . .and give me someone to keep me accountable.*

Charles Spurgeon

FALSE ALARM AND REAL TRAGEDY

> *The LORD is close to the brokenhearted and*
> *saves those who are crushed in spirit.*
> PSALM 34:18 NIV

Under the leadership of Charles Spurgeon, New Park Street Chapel grew to overflowing. To accommodate more people, the congregation moved up to Exeter Hall for a time before planning services at the enormous Surrey Music Hall.

The idea of holding church in a hall built for amusement was enough to make some churchgoers stay home. It was well they did. In the very first service, Sunday, October 19, 1856, tragedy struck.

Ten thousand people listened to an opening Bible reading, after which Spurgeon paused to pray. In the silence, someone shouted "Fire!" Toward the back of the hall, panic ensued. Seven people were trampled and killed.

There had been no fire. Some speculated that pickpockets incited the panic, hoping to grab wallets in the melee.

Spurgeon, only twenty-two at the time, was understandably shaken by the experience. But he did not abandon his ministry, and the world is better for the decades of solid Bible lessons he produced, which many still study today.

When tragedy strikes, we have the opportunity to show God's power by staying true to His calling. How might your faithfulness affect your world?

> *Father, lend me Your strength when I am*
> *weak, and Your joy when I have none.*

TRAVELING EVANGELIST

> *You see, we don't go around preaching about*
> *ourselves. We preach that Jesus Christ is Lord, and*
> *we ourselves are your servants for Jesus' sake.*
> 2 CORINTHIANS 4:5 NLT

In the beginning, crowds watched Billy Sunday play baseball. Later, people went out to see a prancing preacher.

After Billy's first sermon, a reporter wrote, "Center fielder Billy Sunday made a three-base hit at Farwell Hall last night. There is no other way to express the success of his first appearance as an evangelist in Chicago." Another time, he was described as a "whirling dervish that pranced and cavorted and strode and bounded and pounded all over his platform." Billy was known for his blunt speaking style, with one-liners such as "going to church doesn't make you a Christian any more than going to a garage makes you an automobile."

Billy used his baseball notoriety and his rousing communication style to draw people in and share the gospel. He was unique, but God has given each of us unique talents and characteristics for His service. Do you know yours? If not, ask your pastor or a wise Christian friend to help you discover them.

> *Father, show me how I might use my status,*
> *position, or job to share Christ with the lost.*

UNCERTAINTY AND STRUGGLE

Though they stumble, they will never fall,
or the LORD holds them by the hand.
PSALM 37:24 NLT

The formation of the Chinese Evangelization Society was based on the word of one person who reported that China was ripe for a Christian harvest. Hudson Taylor would soon find that wasn't the case. Missionary success in China would require much more than merely changing his western clothes to fit in.

In less than two years, the society cut funds to all missionaries in China. Hudson, undeterred, resigned from the organization. His medical supplies, being stored in Shanghai, were lost in a fire. On his way to the city of Ningbo, he was robbed of almost everything he owned.

Sometimes, it seems that everything that can go wrong does go wrong, that everywhere we turn ends up as a dead end. The fact is that following Jesus can be filled with uncertainty and struggle.

Thankfully, we know from scripture that God loves us—so much that He knows the number of hairs on our heads! In His own way and time, God provided everything that Hudson Taylor needed, including a wife. He will provide for us too.

Father, help me to continue serving You,
even when I feel like giving up.

WRITING ON THE RUN

> *"If anyone will not welcome you or listen*
> *to your words, leave that home or town*
> *and shake the dust off your feet."*
> MATTHEW 10:14 NIV

As William Tyndale's book *The Obedience of a Christian Man* changed the political landscape of England, so his translation of the Bible into English changed the church forever.

In 1523, at age twenty-nine, Tyndale went to London and formally requested the help of Bishop Cuthbert Tunstall to begin translation work. Tunstall turned Tyndale away at the door. A year later, Tyndale left England for the continent, eventually arriving at Worms, where Martin Luther published his German New Testament. By 1526, Tyndale's English New Testament had been published and was quietly smuggled into England.

Tyndale tried to work with the official church but was turned away. Instead of quitting, though, he pressed ahead, doing God's will on the way. If Tyndale hadn't continued his work, the Reformation might have passed England by.

When you hit roadblocks to your Christian calling, don't quit! Adjust course and keep working. Find out what God can do with a man who presses forward when the world tries to stop him.

Lord, show me the work You want me to do. Give me
the strength and bravery to accomplish Your will.

HEART STRANGELY WARMED

*He is the atoning sacrifice for our sins, and not only
for ours but also for the sins of the whole world.*
1 JOHN 2:2 NIV

John Wesley kept a journal after college. It contained an elaborate record of every hour each day, measuring his devotion to God on a scale of one to nine. But no matter how fierce his devotion, Wesley never felt he had attained salvation. One day, an encounter with biblical truth changed his life.

"In the evening, I went very unwillingly to a society in Aldersgate Street, where one was reading Luther's preface to the Epistle to the Romans," Wesley recalled. "About a quarter before nine, while he was describing the change which God works in the heart through faith in Christ, I felt my heart strangely warmed. I felt I did trust in Christ, Christ alone for salvation, and an assurance was given that he had taken away my sins, even mine, and saved me from the law of sin and death."

It's part of our fallen nature for humans to want to save themselves. But we dare not forget what Jesus did. He took every wrong we have ever done (or will do), paying their price through His death and resurrection. The only appropriate response is grateful acceptance.

*Father, I thank You that no matter what,
I cannot out-sin Your grace.*

ON THE WRONG SIDE OF THE SLAVERY DEBATE

Were you a slave when you were called?
Don't let it trouble you—although if you
can gain your freedom, do so.
1 CORINTHIANS 7:21 NIV

When it came to preaching, George Whitefield was almost super-human. It was estimated that before he died, 80 percent of American colonists had heard him preach in person.

But the man wasn't perfect. When an orphanage he had started in Georgia cost more than he initially planned, Whitefield pushed for the colony to legalize slavery for cheaper labor. Though he advocated for the humane treatment of slaves and was one of the first itinerant preachers to preach to them, we cannot overlook his acceptance of the idea of human bondage.

Unfortunately, such blind spots are common among Christians. We may be doing great work for the Lord yet all the while missing an issue like Whitefield had with slavery. The only way to see a blind spot is to pray for the Holy Spirit to make it plain. Then be ready for Him to use someone you know to point it out.

Lord, if there are things in my life that don't glorify
You, help me see them. I want Your Spirit to bring
me into complete alignment with Your will.

ABOLITIONIST OPPOSITION

*We also pray that you will be strengthened with all
his glorious power so you will have all the endurance
and patience you need. May you be filled with joy.*
COLOSSIANS 1:11 NLT

As William Wilberforce began his mission to abolish slavery, he sincerely believed it would be a swift victory. In Parliament in 1789, he introduced twelve resolutions against the slave trade only to have them circumvented by sly legal means.

Over the next seventeen years, William's bills were defeated eight different times. Still, he was undeterred. When his opponents, some of whom benefited greatly by the slave trade, realized he was never going to give up, they turned on him.

The barrage of personal and political opposition was so strong that one friend commented he would not be surprised if he read about William's death by being, "carbonated [broiled] by Indian planters, barbecued by African merchants, and eaten by Guinea captains."

Don't be surprised when people oppose your good efforts—even the simplest things done for Jesus' sake. Remember, He promised that we would encounter trouble when we follow Him. . .but also that He overcomes the world (John 16:33).

*Father, whatever oppression I endure
for Your name, help me stand firm in the
convictions You have laid on my heart.*

READY TO DEFEND CONVICTIONS

Whatsoever thy hand findeth to do, do it with thy might; for there is no work, nor device, nor knowledge, nor wisdom, in the grave, whither thou goest.
ECCLESIASTES 9:10 KJV

In the 1300s, John Wycliffe's dissenting activities did not sit well with church leaders in Rome. His books challenged the legitimacy of the papacy. His idea that scripture is the ultimate authority was considered subversive. His recommendation that England—preparing for a possible attack by France—not send money to Rome was the last straw.

Wycliffe was summoned to London and charged with numerous counts of heresy. Before the hearing got underway, however, a fight broke out between church representatives and Wycliffe's supporters. The meeting ended without a conviction, but Pope Gregory XI soon issued five papal bulls—official proclamations—deeming Wycliffe "the master of errors." Undeterred, in a later hearing before the archbishop, Wycliffe declared, "I am ready to defend my convictions even unto death. I have followed the sacred scriptures and the holy doctors."

John Wycliffe was willing to put his life in peril because he believed so strongly in the Bible's authority. What is your ultimate source of authority?

Father, give me the conviction to believe Your Word, and the courage always to stand up for it.

Dietrich Bonhoeffer

DOUBLE AGENT

> *The king of Egypt summoned the midwives and asked them, "Why have you done this? Why have you let the boys live?" The midwives answered Pharaoh, "Hebrew women are not like Egyptian women; they are vigorous and give birth before the midwives arrive." So God was kind to the midwives and the people increased.*
> EXODUS 1:18–20 NIV

With the Nazis' discovery of the underground seminary of Finkenwalde, Dietrich Bonhoeffer could no longer teach young German pastors. So he did something no one expected: he signed up with the military intelligence service, the Abwehr.

A brother-in-law, already part of the service, brought Bonhoeffer into the Abwehr by arguing his contacts throughout European churches would be helpful to Germany. He was supposed to travel to church conferences, collecting intelligence on the countries and people he encountered. In reality, Bonhoeffer used his travels to establish contacts to help Jewish people escape Nazi oppression.

Serving as a double agent is inherently dishonest, seemingly out of line with God's Word. But, as with the Hebrew midwives Shiphrah and Puah, who resisted the Pharaoh's order to drown newborns, the larger issue of human life takes precedence. If we're ever called to make such choices, let's be sure they're bathed in deep Bible study and prayer.

Father, may my choices always honor You and help the innocent.

GOD'S FAITHFUL PROVISION

*Because of the LORD's great love we are not
consumed, for his compassions never fail. They are
new every morning; great is your faithfulness.*
LAMENTATIONS 3:22–23 NIV

After Brother Andrew completed two years at Worldwide Evangelisation Crusade Bible College in Glasgow Scotland, he was unsure of his next move. His training, however, taught him that God would provide—and He did.

Feeling drawn to a communist youth rally in Poland, Andrew did not hesitate to clearly state his intention of sharing the gospel of Jesus Christ. Though closed to Christianity, the Polish government miraculously allowed him to attend.

This way of living by faith and trusting in God, rather than relying on his own clever plans, would form the foundation of all Brother Andrew's endeavors. Several decades later, his active faith would be described by *Christianity Today* magazine: "Brother Andrew is a doer. While most Christians put out fleeces, he would already be on the plane, facing danger, finding a way into some place others describe as 'closed.' "

Over the decades, God provided for Brother Andrew. He is always faithful to His people, even those who give their lives for Jesus. They just get to enjoy His presence sooner.

*Father, You are faithful to me.
Help me always to be faithful to You!*

PREACHER IN PRISON

> *But Peter and John replied, "Which is right in*
> *God's eyes: to listen to you, or to him? You be*
> *the judges! As for us, we cannot help speaking*
> *about what we have seen and heard."*
> ACTS 4:19–20 NIV

After his conversion, the frivolous sinner John Bunyan became a preacher and family man. When his first wife died in 1658, Bunyan remarried so his four children—the oldest of whom was blind—would have a mother. She was soon the only parent they had at home.

Why? Because Bunyan was charged with preaching unlawfully to groups outside the parish church. In 1661, he was locked up in the county jail.

The "crime" was punishable by three months' imprisonment followed by banishment or even execution if the person kept preaching unlawfully. Bunyan didn't stop. He ultimately spent twelve years in prison, supporting his family by making shoelaces. He also used his time to write.

Trusting God doesn't always make our lives easier. Bunyan himself experienced trouble, and his whole family suffered because of the stand he took. But if he hadn't spent that time in jail, we might not have one of the most influential Christian books of all time: *The Pilgrim's Progress*.

> *Lord, give me the courage to do what is right,*
> *even if it brings suffering in this life.*

A VEHEMENT REQUEST

> *Trust in the LORD with all thine heart; and lean not unto thine own understanding. In all thy ways acknowledge him, and he shall direct thy paths.*
> PROVERBS 3:5–6 KJV

After publishing the *Institutes of the Christian Religion*, John Calvin became a man on the run. The Catholic church in France was persecuting Protestants, going as far as to burn some at the stake. Soon, Calvin left France for good.

He crossed the border into Switzerland with a brother, sister, and two friends with plans to stay in Geneva for one night before continuing their journey. While there, a local church leader, William Farel, discovered the writer of "The Institutes" was in town and begged Calvin to stay. He was reluctant until Farel warned that God would ruin Calvin's scholarly pursuits if he moved on.

Later, John would write, "I felt as if God from heaven had laid His mighty hand upon me to stop me in my course—and I was so terror stricken that I did not continue my journey."

Sometimes our plans come up against massive roadblocks, and we're not sure what to do next. Those are the times we weigh the input of scripture, Christian friends, and our own conscience as directed by the Holy Spirit. In His own time, God will show us the path.

> *Father as I travel the road of faith, help me to heed Your call, no matter what my plans are.*

NEVER ALONE

If we are unfaithful, he remains faithful,
for he cannot deny who he is.
2 TIMOTHY 2:13 NLT

In 1793, William Carey, his family, and physician John Thomas set sail for India determined to share Christ. Though British, the group journeyed aboard a Dutch vessel, as the powerful British East India Company (which Thomas served) was unsupportive of their missionary endeavors.

The group settled in a British colony, where William and John took jobs managing indigo factories. Having severely underestimated their expenses, they needed to earn money. Within a few short years, the situation grew worse. Thomas abandoned the group and Carey caught malaria. One of his sons died and his wife began the onset of mental illness.

At one point, Carey wrote in his journal, "I have had hurrying up and down; a five month's imprisonment with carnal men on board the ship. . .my colleague separated from me; long delays, and few opportunities for social worship. . .no earthly thing to depend upon." But, like a psalm writer, he ended hopefully: "Well, I have God, and His Word is sure."

We all have times in life when we feel alone—perhaps even abandoned. William Carey turned to scripture for encouragement. You can too.

Father, when everything seems to collapse around
me, I trust Your Word, which says You are faithful.

ON PEANUTS

"Call to me and I will answer you and tell you great
and unsearchable things you do not know."
JEREMIAH 33:3 NIV

George Washington Carver is best remembered for promoting peanuts. Here's a story he frequently told:

"One day I went into my laboratory and said, 'Dear Mr. Creator, please tell me what the universe was made for.' The Great Creator answered, 'You want to know too much for that little mind of yours. Ask something more your size, little man.' Then I asked, 'Please, Mr. Creator, tell me what man was made for.' Again the Great Creator replied, 'You are still asking too much.' So then I asked, 'Please, Mr. Creator, will you tell me why the peanut was made?' 'That's better,' God answered, 'what do you want to know about the peanut?' "

In 1920, Carver famously exhibited 145 ways to use the peanut to a group of growers, then went before Congress as an expert witness to plead on behalf of the peanut industry. His insights helped farmers enrich their soil and keep their farms.

By listening to God, George Washington Carver helped others. What is God telling you today? How are you using that to help the people around you?

Lord, show me what You want me to
know so I can do the most good.

THE EXTRA MILE

> *"If anyone forces you to go one mile,*
> *go with them two miles."*
> MATTHEW 5:41 NIV

Frederick Douglass believed that if you had power or influence, you should use it to create positive change. When some people questioned whether he'd really been a slave, he wrote an autobiography. When he faced opposition, he spoke out more. He used every opportunity to call attention to the injustice of slavery.

"The slave auctioneer's bell and the churchgoing bell chime in with each other, and the bitter cries of the heartbroken slave are drowned in the religious shouts of his pious master," he wrote in *Narrative of the Life of Frederick Douglass, an American Slave*. "Revivals of religion and revivals in the slave trade go hand in hand."

He would repeat lines of his speeches, hoping they would turn into catchphrases, such as, "Between the Christianity of this land, and the Christianity of Christ, I recognize the widest possible difference." He was urging his audience to look closer at the true, biblical Jesus.

Christ commanded His followers to do more than expected when dealing with other people. As a former slave, Frederick Douglass had to. As a free man in the twenty-first century, will you?

Lord, please help me to "go the extra mile"
for others, as a form of worship to You.

DISMISSED

And we know that all things work together
for good to them that love God, to them who
are the called according to his purpose.
ROMANS 8:28 KJV

Though he would become widely known for his role in the Great Awakening, Jonathan Edwards was committed to the spiritual health of his own church in Northampton, Massachusetts. But he was not always appreciated there.

The most divisive issue regarded the Lord's Supper. Edwards believed the sacrament was reserved for church members in good standing who had made a profession of faith within the church. The church's founder (who was Edwards' own grandfather) had taught that communion was an ordinance of conversion, so it didn't matter whether individuals made a profession of faith. In the end, the church dismissed Edwards.

As Christians, we'll always be at odds with the world. But there will even be times when our beliefs and practices will be questioned by fellow believers. Instead of allowing these disagreements to turn us away from God, let's follow in the footsteps of Jonathan Edwards, who went on to serve another church, preach to native Americans, write, and lead what came to be known as Princeton University.

Lord, when I face opposition, whether it is from the
world or from Your people, let me stay faithful to You.

OPERATION WAODANI

> *Let us not become weary in doing good, for at the*
> *proper time we will reap a harvest if we do not give up.*
> GALATIANS 6:9 NIV

Jim Elliot longed to introduce a remote Ecuadorian tribe to Jesus. So he lined up a missionary pilot and three other Christians to join him on his quest to reach the Waodani. Now, however, they faced a great challenge.

The jungle landscape provided no place to land. And even if they could set their plane down, the Waodani were aggressive, willing to kill to defend their territory. If Jim and his team landed unannounced, they might ruin their mission. . .or worse.

Then someone thought of the perfect introduction. They put a bucket on a long rope, and lowered gifts from their circling plane. The natives took the gifts, and after a few days, the pilot discovered a straight section of river he could land on.

Whether we're in missionary service or just being Christians in everyday life, we'll run into obstructions and frustrations. But quitting is not an option. The question is, how will we adapt and overcome? Step one: pray. Start with the words below:

> *Lord, when I am stuck in life show me*
> *the way that I do not see.*

GENERAL IN THE SALVATION ARMY

Put on salvation as your helmet, and take the
sword of the Spirit, which is the word of God.
EPHESIANS 6:17 NLT

Within ten years of founding the East London Christian Mission in 1865, William and Catherine Booth had gathered over a thousand volunteers. Then in 1878 came a name change for the organization.

Reviewing a proof copy of the group's annual report, William read aloud, "the Christian Mission is a volunteer army." His son Bramwell balked at the line saying, "Volunteer? I'm no volunteer. I'm a regular!" William scratched out the word *volunteer* and wrote *salvation* in its place.

Thus, the Salvation Army was born. A military structure and new uniforms followed. Converts became known as Salvationists and by 1885, their ranks had swelled to more than a quarter million.

Whether or not you've ever been part of the Salvation Army, as a Christian you are part of God's army. And you aren't a volunteer, you're a regular! Put on your armor, pick up your sword, and fight to bring others to peace.

Lord, help me follow your orders and example well.
Train my hands to battle the unseen powers against me.

Billy Graham

DOUBTING REVIVALIST

All glory to the only wise God,
through Jesus Christ, forever. Amen.
ROMANS 16:27 NLT

By the time he was in his early thirties, word was spreading about Billy Graham. He was invited to preach at a revival in Los Angeles.

Before the event, Billy discussed his plans on Stuart Hamblen's radio show. That publicity sparked the interest of media magnate William Randolph Hearst, who covered the revival in his newspapers.

Initially planned for three weeks, the revival stretched to eight. God used Billy's preaching to reach over 350,000 people, including Hamblen, television star Harvey Fritts, mobster Jim Vaus, and Olympian and World War II prisoner of war Louis Zamperini. But the event almost didn't happen.

Going into the crusade, Billy Graham was struggling with doubts, about the Bible and his calling. But he stepped up and did his best. "The Los Angeles Crusade has humbled and driven me to my knees as never before," Graham said. "People have wanted to praise me for what happened at Los Angeles during eight blessed weeks [but] God deserves all the glory."

When you are willing to set aside doubt and do your best for God, just watch and see how He proves Himself!

Lord, when I have doubts, let me see Your
power. Humble me and keep me faithful.

Hear counsel, and receive instruction,
that thou mayest be wise in thy latter end.
PROVERBS 19:20 KJV

Between the early 1930s and late 1949, C. S. Lewis ("Jack," as his friends called him) belonged to an informal literary group called the Inklings. One meeting might include J. R. R. Tolkien reading a chapter from *The Lord of the Rings*, while another would feature a paper on the ethics of cannibalism.

Jack's brother Warren described an Inklings meeting in his introduction to the book *Letters of C. S. Lewis*: "The ritual of an Inklings was unvarying. When half a dozen or so had arrived, tea would be produced, and then when pipes were well alight Jack would say, 'Well, has nobody got anything to read us?' Out would come a manuscript, and we would settle down to sit in judgement upon it—real unbiased judgement, too, since we were no mutual admiration society: praise for good work was unstinted, but censure for bad work—or even not-so-good work—was often brutally frank."

We all enjoy praise, but criticism can be tougher to swallow. Yet honest feedback from true friends can help us become better people. Do you have wise counsel in your life? Be sure to take it to heart.

Lord, may I trust rebukes from my
friends as much as their praise.

NOT FOR SALE

*Keep your lives free from the love of money and be
content with what you have, because God has said,
"Never will I leave you; never will I forsake you."*
HEBREWS 13:5 NIV

Eric Liddell's Olympic victory has been recounted on both film and paper. In the book *For the Glory*, British author Duncan Hamilton writes about Eric's rise to stardom after winning the 400-meter gold medal in 1924. Though he could have used his newly won fame for personal benefit, Hamilton writes that Liddell "wasn't for sale at any price."

When the Olympics were over, Eric packed his bags and moved to China, the land of his birth. There, he took up the "family business" of missionary work. He spent time teaching at an Anglo-Chinese college in Tientsin before hitting the road to evangelize rural China. Eric traveled by foot or used a bike to share the love of Jesus with the Chinese.

It's easy to get caught up in our own personal successes, especially if they're as big as Eric Liddell's. But we can thank God for the great example this humble missionary provides—of steadfast resolve to follow God's calling for life.

*Lord, help me to always focus on what You would
have me do, not on how I can get what I want.*

NOT A DUMPY SORT OF MAN

*And whatsoever ye do, do it heartily,
as to the Lord, and not unto men.*
COLOSSIANS 3:23 KJV

After leaving his mission post, David Livingstone turned his attention to opening travel routes to Africa's interior. While back in England to raise interest in Africa's welfare, he was accused of failing as a missionary.

Livingstone answered, "Nowhere have I ever appeared as anything else but a servant of God, who has simply followed the leadings of His hand. My views of what is missionary duty are not so contracted as those whose ideal is a dumpy sort of man with a Bible under his arm. I have labored in bricks and mortar, at the forge and carpenter's bench, as well as in preaching and medical practice."

Livingstone believed his abilities were of better use for Christ by paving the way for other evangelizers to follow in his path. As such, he worked toward spreading the gospel in his own way.

We've all been called to be missionaries, whether to a foreign country or in our own daily jobs. Remember, a missionary isn't just a "dumpy sort of man with a Bible under his arm." It's you, as you represent your Lord.

Lord, take my work and use it for Your glory.

EXCOMMUNICATED

Warn a divisive person once, and then warn them a second time. After that, have nothing to do with them.
TITUS 3:10 NIV

In the early church, the apostles recommended excommunication to bring a church member to repentance. The church was not to speak to, have business dealings with, or even eat with the offending person.

After Martin Luther published the *Ninety-Five Theses*, he was warned by the Catholic church to recant lest he be excommunicated. When Luther was finally served with the official papal bull banishing him, he burned it. His response: "My articles are called 'respectively some heretical, some erroneous, some scandalous,' which is as much to say, 'We don't know which are which.' O meticulous ignorance!"

In his reaction, Martin Luther recognized only God's authority, and he essentially excommunicated the Catholic church in return. His view that Rome was dividing believers from God fueled the Reformation.

God wants unity among believers (see, for example, John 17:11, 21–22), but not at the cost of truth (see, for example, Jude 3–4). Martin Luther wore his excommunication from a corrupt church as a badge of honor. May we follow his example, carefully—division is never to be taken lightly.

Lord, give me unity with my siblings in Christ, and boldness to stand against falsehood.

DOING NEW THINGS

*Obviously, I'm not trying to win the approval
of people, but of God. If pleasing people were
my goal, I would not be Christ's servant.*
GALATIANS 1:10 NLT

Have you ever let inexperience keep you from trying something new? It's embarrassing to attempt something only to fail. But when that frightening new thing is something you *need* to do, remember this: the only opinion that matters is God's.

In the aftermath of the Great Chicago Fire, D. L. Moody left his ministry in Chicago and became a traveling evangelist. While preaching in Great Britain, he once said, "I know perfectly well that, wherever I go and preach, there are many better preachers known and heard than I am; all that I can say about it is that the Lord uses me."

Though criticized by the others for his unpolished delivery—one critic claimed Moody could pronounce "Nebuchadnezzar" in two syllables—his preaching drew people in and pointed them to Christ.

Are you considering some new endeavor? As long as you're doing it to please God instead of men, step out boldly. What does it matter if the world considers you a fool, if you're doing God's will?

*Lord, don't let my fear of failure keep
me from doing Your will.*

FINDING STEPHEN MERRITT

> *"Give to those who ask, and don't turn away
> from those who want to borrow."*
> MATTHEW 5:42 NLT

Samuel Morris sailed from Africa to New York in 1891. He carried almost nothing but a name, provided by a missionary, of a man who might help him. There were roughly 1.7 million people living in New York City at the time.

At the docks, Morris asked the first man he met, "Where's Stephen Merritt?"

"I know him," the man replied. "I'll take you to him for a dollar."

"All right," said Samuel, though he had not a cent.

Arriving just as Merritt was stepping out, Morris said, "I am Samuel Morris; I've just come from Africa to talk with you about the Holy Ghost."

Merritt directed the young man to a soup kitchen and said they would connect later. Meanwhile, Morris's guide was demanding his dollar.

"Oh," Samuel said, "Stephen Merritt pays my bills now." And Merritt passed a dollar along.

As Christians, we can make a similarly audacious claim—we have someone who pays our bills. God has promised to take care of our needs, and we in turn are called to take care of others.

Lord, may I be as giving to others as You have been to me.

THE GOLDEN RULE

> *"Do to others whatever you would like them
> to do to you. This is the essence of all that is
> taught in the law and the prophets."*
> MATTHEW 7:12 NLT

So you're trying to do the right thing. . .and someone complains. Ugh! Why does it often seem that no good deed goes unpunished?

Perhaps God is giving you a chance to demonstrate Jesus' Golden Rule. That's how George Müller viewed complaints from the neighbors of his orphanage. They felt "inconvenienced" by the "noise of the children during playtime." Müller admitted that they had a point, writing, "It would probably give me a headache if I lived next door to the Orphan Houses." His response? "I therefore should do to others as I want them to do for me."

Not surprisingly, Müller immediately began praying—and before long, God unveiled a plan for a large complex in the country. By the time he died in 1898, Müller had served more than *ten thousand* orphans. Would he have had such an impact if he had chosen to argue with the neighbors in 1845?

The Golden Rule benefits everyone.

---

*Lord Jesus, please give me Your quiet grace when others
are difficult. Help me to follow Your Golden Rule.*

MISSIONARY TO THE [ART] WORLD

And let the beauty of the LORD our God be upon us:
and establish thou the work of our hands upon us.
PSALM 90:17 KJV

Christians today know Oswald Chambers' name for the beloved daily devotional *My Utmost for His Highest.* But he didn't write the book—his wife, Biddy, compiled 365 daily readings from sermons and lessons he delivered to various audiences in the early twentieth century.

Born in Scotland in 1874, the young Chambers showed a strong artistic bent. As a teen, he wanted to "strike for the redemption of the Aesthetic Kingdom—Music and Art and Poetry—or rather, the proving of Christ's redemption of it." Chambers dreamed of being God's missionary to the art world.

As it turned out, the Lord wanted Chambers to serve a larger world. He would preach and teach throughout the United Kingdom, North America, Japan, and the Middle East, where he served soldiers of the British Empire fighting the Great War—what we call World War I.

Oswald Chambers released his aesthetic dreams with difficulty, but God was clearly directing him to bigger and better things. Would he be remembered today had he become an artist? Trust that God's ways are always best.

───────────────────

Lord God, lead me in Your ways and use me for Your glory.

CLEAVING TO DUST

> *But encourage one another daily, as long as*
> *it is called "Today," so that none of you may*
> *be hardened by sin's deceitfulness.*
> HEBREWS 3:13 NIV

Have you ever had a moment of such spiritual clarity you were sure life would change forever? How long did that last? Unfortunately, it can be difficult to sustain a spiritual fervor when life returns to routine.

After being twice rescued—once from servitude to a slave trader in 1747, and once from shipwreck in 1748—John Newton gave his life to God. "I had learned to pray. I set some value upon the word of God, and was no longer a libertine," he said later, "but my soul still cleaved to the dust."

Until 1754, Newton's work was captaining vessels for the slave trade. His conversion was genuine, but his heart often went astray. Not until a stroke permanently kept him from seafaring did John Newton step into a more reputable way of life.

When God gives us spiritual clarity, we should immediately act on that insight. Don't waste time in old activities or worrying about a return to sinful ways. Instead, surround yourself with godly people who can hold you accountable when life returns to routine. Never become hardened by sin's deceitfulness.

> *Lord, give me clarity and surround me with*
> *people who will keep me from sin.*

TRANSFORMATIONAL POWER

*I have been crucified with Christ and I no longer
live, but Christ lives in me. The life I now live
in the body, I live by faith in the Son of God,
who loved me and gave himself for me.*
GALATIANS 2:20 NIV

By 1970, Luis Palau was holding international evangelistic crusades. In El Salvador's capital, Luis followed each day's crusade with an appearance on a live televised counseling program. Returning to his hotel one night after 1:45 a.m., he was met by a man who had seen the broadcast.

The well-known psychologist confessed to alcoholism and numerous infidelities. He asked Luis, "Is there any hope of change for a hypocrite like me?"

Palau told the man about the transformational power of Christ. There in the hotel lobby, he accepted Jesus as Lord.

A week later, the psychologist called in to the counseling program to say his life was completely different—and now his wife wanted to talk to Luis. And Palau led her to Christ on live television.

He accomplished many great things, but Luis Palau was not the source of people's life change—God was. And when you need change, He'll help you too. Just ask.

*Lord, help me to live without hypocrisy.
Make me fully devoted to You.*

FROM LAY MONK TO BISHOP

He guides me along the right paths for his name's sake.
PSALM 23:3 NIV

After giving his entire life to Christ, Augustine lost his mother, son, and closest friend. But these losses, rather than ruining his newfound faith in Jesus, instead deepened it. He and his friends developed a community in Thagaste, his hometown, devoted to prayer and the study of scripture.

God had larger plans for Augustine. When he visited Hippo and attended a church service there, the bishop, Valerius, recognized the intellectual convert and changed his message to describe a dire need for priests in Hippo. Augustine was ushered forward by the crowd and, reluctantly, accepted ordination.

Though he preferred to remain a lay monk, Augustine heeded God's call to become a public figure in the church. First a priest, then a bishop when Valerius died. . .and before long, Augustine would be a pivotal figure in the entire Christian faith.

Have you ever been reluctant to serve God in some capacity? Consider the example of Augustine and see what your obedience might accomplish.

---

*Father, I pray that You will prepare my
heart to act whenever You call.*

MAKING PEOPLE LISTEN

"Whoever has ears, let them hear."
MATTHEW 11:15 NIV

With popularity often comes criticism. So while some called Charles Spurgeon the "Prince of Preachers," others referred to him as the "Pulpit Buffoon." Both titles stemmed from Spurgeon's willingness to preach in a manner unbefitting the upper classes to which most aspired.

"I am neither eloquent nor learned," wrote Spurgeon to one newspaper editor, "but the Head of the Church has given me sympathy with the masses, love to the poor, and the means of winning the attention of the ignorant and unenlightened. . . . I am perhaps vulgar, and so on, but it is not intentional, save that I *must* and *will* make the people listen. My firm conviction is that we have quite enough *polite* preachers, and that 'the many' require a change. God has owned me to the most degraded and off-cast; let others serve their class; these are mine, and to them I must keep."

Spurgeon didn't preach to please the upper classes, and neither did Jesus. Are you letting others' judgment keep you from sharing the gospel? If we are more concerned with our standing in society than with kneeling before the cross, our posture needs correction.

Lord, don't let me worry about social standing when I should be spreading Your gospel to everyone who will listen.

CHAMPION OF SOCIAL REFORM

*"The King will reply, 'Truly I tell you, whatever
you did for one of the least of these brothers
and sisters of mine, you did for me.' "*
MATTHEW 25:40 NIV

If you had attended one of Billy Sunday's evangelistic speaking engagements, you would have seen a wildly enthusiastic preacher. You would also have heard something unusual. While most American evangelists steered clear of social issues, Billy Sunday waded right in.

He was a supporter of women's suffrage. When he toured the deep south, he welcomed the African American community. He supported Roman Catholics, who he counted as fellow Christians, and Jews. He also helped to raise money in support of American troops in the Great War (what we know as World War I).

For Billy Sunday, the gospel was more than just a change of belief—it affected all of life. He lived the truth of James 2:26 (NIV): "As the body without the spirit is dead, so faith without deeds is dead."

As believers in Christ, we are called to share the gospel *and* assist people in need. If an individual or organization could benefit from your help, don't hesitate to join in for Jesus' sake.

---

*Father, move my heart toward action.
Show me where I can serve.*

GOD'S RESPONSIBILITIES

When doubts filled my mind, your comfort
gave me renewed hope and cheer.
PSALM 94:19 NLT

After several years in China, Hudson Taylor became severely ill. He reluctantly left his church of twenty-one members and traveled back to England to recover.

At home, Hudson worked harder than ever. He campaigned for more missionaries for China, continued translating the Bible into Chinese, studied to become a midwife, wrote books, and drafted a plan for a new missionary organization.

Soon, Taylor was discouraged and burned out. He wrote in his diary that he felt he was losing his mind. A friend encouraged him to take a retreat at the coast to rest.

"There the Lord conquered my unbelief," Taylor would say, "and I surrendered myself to God for this service. I told Him that all responsibility as to the issues and consequences must rest with Him; that as His servant it was mine to obey and to follow Him."

If you are burned out and weary, find a place to rest and connect with God. Remember, He has charge over the outcome of His plans. Our job is simply to trust and obey.

Father, I come to find rest in You.
Fill me with peace and direction.

FINANCED BY ENEMIES

"You intended to harm me, but God intended it for good to accomplish what is now being done, the saving of many lives."
GENESIS 50:20 NIV

When William Tyndale's English translation of the New Testament was smuggled into Britain, Bishop Tunstall of London—whom Tyndale had originally asked for help—outlawed the book. Tunstall bought and burned copies as he found them.

Tyndale remarked, "In burning the New Testament they did none other thing than that I looked for. No more shall they do if they burn me also, if it be God's will, it shall so be. In translating the New Testament I did my duty, and so do I now, and will do as much more as God hath ordained me to do."

Tyndale himself *would* eventually be burned. But for a time his translation work was actually financed by those buying his New Testaments to destroy them.

God can use even the destruction of Bibles to further the spread of His Word. Nothing is beyond His capabilities. If something is bothering you today, consider God's larger perspective . . .and trust Him to do what is best.

Lord, when I am discouraged, give me Your eyes and the bravery to continue.

PREACHING OUTDOORS

*Now when Jesus saw the crowds, he went up
on a mountainside and sat down. His disciples
came to him, and he began to teach them.*
MATTHEW 5:1–2 NIV

After John Wesley's conversion at Aldersgate, he was asked to help a friend who was preaching to London's working-class poor. The friend was the famed evangelist George Whitefield, who was experiencing an overwhelming response to his ministry.

Wesley hesitated to join Whitefield for two reasons. First, he did not trust Whitefield's dramatic preaching style. Second, Wesley felt Whitefield lacked decorum by preaching outdoors. However, after finally agreeing to help Whitefield, Wesley found that he enjoyed teaching outside.

Perhaps he'd forgotten that one of Jesus' most famous sermons, the Sermon on the Mount, was delivered on a hillside! Surely the Lord is the best example of acceptable behavior for His followers.

Sometimes we encounter situations in our Christian life that make us uncomfortable. At those times, it's wise to stop and ask ourselves if the discomfort is due to a moral concern or simply our unfamiliarity with a method or style. If the latter, give the thing a try—you might find, like John Wesley did, that you enjoy it.

*Father, examine my heart. Show me where my
prejudices intrude on my service to Jesus.*

ORIGINAL AMERICAN CELEBRITY

> *"How can you believe since you accept
> glory from one another but do not seek the
> glory that comes from the only God?"*
> JOHN 5:44 NIV

George Whitefield crossed the Atlantic thirteen times, traveled the length of America's eastern seaboard, and preached the whole while. Aside from British royalty, his name was more readily recognized than any other person's in America—even Whitefield's friend Benjamin Franklin.

In fact, without Whitefield, the American colonies might not have broken away from England when they did. According to Jerome Mahaffey, author of *The Accidental Revolutionary: George Whitefield and the Creation of America*, "of all the colonial leaders and their ideas, if you remove Whitefield and his contribution, no one else had the message, popularity, and influence to shape American colonists into people who could declare independence."

Whitefield could have leveraged his popularity to gain a leadership role in this new nation. But that wasn't the mission God gave him. He kept preaching, pointing people to Jesus.

If you're ever tempted to seek and use popularity for something other than God's glory, your success is bound to be temporary. Keep an eternal perspective, remembering that the only approval you need is God's.

---

*Lord, when I am tempted to seek glory for myself,
humble me and help me work for Your glory.*

PRIME MINISTER OF PHILANTHROPISTS

Whoever is kind to the poor lends to the LORD,
and he will reward them for what they have done.
PROVERBS 19:17 NIV

Although the abolition of slavery was William Wilberforce's great calling, another issue reflected the changes he had made in his own life: the reformation of manners. He created a society that was "for the encouragement of piety and virtue; and for the preventing of vice, profaneness, and immorality." It was eventually called the Society for the Suppression of Vice.

This society emphasized helping less-fortunate people who would be prone to the "vices." Wilberforce donated 25 percent of his yearly salary to the poor, in hopes of helping marginalized citizens like chimney sweeps, orphans, and single mothers. He also assisted in forming the Church Missionary Society, the British and Foreign Bible Society, and the Antislavery Society.

William Wilberforce used his wealth and connections to help the forgotten and powerless of eighteenth-century England. How might you give of your time, talents, and finances to help the needy in your community?

Father, today I remember those who are
less fortunate than I am. Show me how I
can give generously of all that I have.

UNDER HOUSE ARREST

Pray also for me, that whenever I speak,
words may be given me so that I will fearlessly
make known the mystery of the gospel.
EPHESIANS 6:19 NIV

John Wycliffe's insistence on biblical accuracy got him in trouble with church authorities in Rome. But the "Great Schism" of 1378, when rival popes were elected, moderated his situation. Wycliffe was simply placed under house arrest, forbidden to travel but allowed to teach at his parish in Lutterworth.

Wycliffe kept poking the bear of Rome, growing bolder as he attacked beliefs for which he could not find a basis in scripture. He argued against transubstantiation, saying, "The bread while becoming by virtue of Christ's words the body of Christ does not cease to be bread." He said that confession to a priest "was not ordered by Christ and was not used by the apostles." And he continued to champion Jesus alone as the way of approaching God. "Trust wholly in Christ; rely altogether on His sufferings; beware of seeking to be justified in any other way than by His righteousness."

There are plenty of biblical interpretations "out there," and many of them sound reasonable. But only by studying scripture ourselves, deeply, can we really know which ones to believe.

Lord, Fill my heart with fire for Your Word.

IN CHAINS FOR CHRIST

*Now I want you to know, brothers and sisters, that
what has happened to me has actually served to
advance the gospel. As a result, it has become
clear throughout the whole palace guard and to
everyone else that I am in chains for Christ.*
PHILIPPIANS 1:12–13 NIV

In the spring of 1943, the Nazis discovered that Dietrich Bonhoeffer
had been helping Jews escape Germany. Branded as a member of
the resistance, he was arrested and taken to Tegel Prison.

Although his opportunity to impact the world narrowed
considerably, Bonhoeffer continued to share the gospel of Jesus
Christ. He explained his faith with those incarcerated with him,
and he wrote letters to his family and friends. Bonhoeffer's letters
were eventually released in book form (*Letters and Papers from
Prison*, first published in 1951).

If you haven't already noticed, life will throw many challenges
your way. In times of trouble and grief, it's easy to become upset
with God. But, as Dietrich Bonhoeffer shows, these times "in
chains" are an opportunity for God to use you to keep carrying
the name of Jesus to your world.

*Lord, build in me a resolve to be faithful. I still want
to serve You when the unexpected happens.*

THE BIBLE-FILLED BEETLE

> *"Indeed, the very hairs of your head are*
> *all numbered. Don't be afraid; you are*
> *worth more than many sparrows."*
> LUKE 12:7 NIV

Brother Andrew was banished from Poland for sharing the gospel, encouraging the church, and distributing Bibles. That only gave him a desire to visit more Communist countries where people were starved for scripture.

Andrew acquired his iconic Volkswagen Beetle and proceeded to smuggle Bibles behind the Iron Curtain. During one endeavor, with a carload of contraband, he watched as car after car was searched at the Romanian border. One car even had its hubcaps removed! Stuck in line, not knowing what to do, Andrew prayed.

God gave him peace, and Andrew was ready to trust Him completely—to the point of placing some Bibles on the passenger seat of his car. When it was Andrew's turn to be searched, the guards looked at his passport for thirty seconds and then miraculously waved him through.

In a moment of panic, Brother Andrew stopped everything and prayed. Are you worried about something today? Stop and pray. God is waiting to listen and answer.

Father, remind me today that nothing is worth
worrying about. You know every sparrow that
falls—and I'm worth much more than a bird!

John Bunyan

A PILGRIM'S JOURNEY

*"You can enter God's Kingdom only through the
narrow gate. The highway to hell is broad, and its
gate is wide for the many who choose that way.
But the gateway to life is very narrow and the
road is difficult, and only a few ever find it."*
MATTHEW 7:13–14 NLT

The Pilgrim's Progress by John Bunyan is one of the earliest English novels, and it hasn't been out of print since first published in 1678.

The book was immediately popular in England, and within three years, it had reached the Puritan colonies in the new world. Since that time, its popularity has hardly waned. According to Christian scholar Leland Ryken, "more than two centuries after its first publication, *The Pilgrim's Progress* ranked just behind the King James Bible as the most important book in evangelical Protestant households." Even today, several dozen editions of the book are available for purchase.

The tale of Christian on the road to Celestial City is one to which every believer can relate. The narrow road isn't easy. Temptations and difficulties conspire to turn you from the right path. But Jesus is more than chief resident of heaven—He is your traveling companion, always ready to draw you back toward Himself. Allow Jesus to accompany you, and you'll arrive safely home.

*Lord, help me to stay on the narrow road.
Keep me from losing my way.*

A PEACEFUL REPRIEVE

*"Stay in this land for a while, and I will be with you
and will bless you. For to you and your descendants
I will give all these lands and will confirm the
oath I swore to your father Abraham."*
GENESIS 26:3 NIV

Before John Calvin even settled in Geneva he was invited to another town. It had been a mere eighteen months since William Farel asked Calvin to stay, and he had felt a deep conviction by the Spirit to oblige.

But then Calvin moved on to Strasbourg, France, where he pastored for three years. While there he married and had children, finding a certain amount of stability. This peaceful period of life enabled him to focus on writing. Calvin completed three books and garnered a reputation as one of the leading Reformers of his day.

Although his early path on the Protestant road was difficult, John Calvin finally enjoyed the blessing of a city where he could live his beliefs openly. God gave Calvin a few years of peace for serving the church and developing his gifts of writing and teaching.

Whenever you find yourself in a peaceful period of life, be grateful—and use that time to sharpen your talents to serve the Lord.

*Lord, no matter where Your path takes me,
help me to serve You wholeheartedly.*

TRIO AND TRANSLATIONS

Though one may be overpowered, two can defend themselves. A cord of three strands is not quickly broken.
ECCLESIASTES 4:12 NIV

William Carey's desire to blaze a missionary trail in India had not gone according to plan. At every step, it seemed, he was met by struggles: the death of his son, the abandonment of his fellow worker, his wife's mental illness. In in the midst of great struggle, he was invited to teach at Fort William College in Serampore, in a Danish region of India.

While things could hardly have been worse for Carey in British India, God gave him many blessings in Serampore. Carey met fellow Christians, enjoyed freedom to share his faith, and obtained financial stability. William also found kinship with William Ward, a printer, and Joshua Marshman, a teacher. Together they became known as the Serampore Trio, and translated the Bible into India's major languages, established orphanages, and sought social reforms, including the elimination of infanticide.

William Carey's friends brought him joy while encouraging him to do great works for God. Do you have any friends like that? If so, thank them. If not, seek some out. For William Carey, they were a life-giving catalyst.

Father, thank You for the encouraging Christians You have placed in my life.

SCIENCE AND THE BIBLE

*Do your best to present yourself to God as one
approved, a worker who does not need to be ashamed
and who correctly handles the word of truth.*
2 TIMOTHY 2:15 NIV

Reconciling his faith with science wasn't a problem for George Washington Carver. And when his students asked him to lead a Bible study once a week, George gladly took on the additional teaching assignment.

Fifty students showed up to George's first Bible class and heard him tell the creation story. Attendance doubled within three months and grew steadily over the thirty years he taught the Bible class. Just as Jesus taught His disciples with agricultural examples, George Washington Carver used creation to teach his students about God.

In a letter from 1930, he wrote, "Nature in its varied forms are the little windows through which God permits me to commune with Him, and to see much of His glory, majesty, and power by simply lifting the curtain and looking in."

George used his passion for science to reach others with his passion for God. What fires your imagination? How can you use that passion to point others to God?

*Creator and Teacher, help me study Your Word and
present Your truth to others in clear, interesting ways.*

MAXIMIZING HIS GIFTS

*Each of you should use whatever gift you have
received to serve others, as faithful stewards
of God's grace in its various forms.*
1 PETER 4:10 NIV

Frederick Douglass was born a slave, but his native intelligence and hunger for learning allowed him to write a bestselling autobiography in 1845. Shortly afterward, in Rochester, New York, he purchased a printing press and started his own newspaper, *The North Star*.

By 1855, Frederick was publishing another book. *My Bondage and My Freedom* an expansion of his original autobiography with an added challenge against racial segregation. He became an advocate for women's rights as well.

When the Civil War broke out, Douglass worked relentlessly to recruit African American men, two of his sons among them. He demanded equal pay for African American soldiers, even sitting down with President Lincoln to discuss the matter. When the war ended, Douglass fought for equal citizenship as he believed the Northern victory would be meaningless without it.

Frederick Douglass had a tremendous gift with words. Whether speaking or writing, he used words to further God's kingdom and help overlooked people gain equal rights.

God has given gifts to all of His followers. Always remember why you have yours—to further His kingdom.

---

*Lord, You have given me gifts. Help me identify
them and use them for Your glory.*

MISSIONARY TO NATIVE AMERICANS

*We can make our plans, but the
LORD determines our steps.*
PROVERBS 16:9 NLT

After being dismissed by his church in Northampton, Massachusetts, Jonathan Edwards could have found another congregation fairly easily. His popularity as a speaker during the Great Awakening brought offers from as far away as Scotland. Instead, he chose to become a missionary to the Native Americans living around Stockbridge.

Edwards preached to his new congregation through an interpreter. He fought the injustice and exploitation committed by white people living among his new flock. And in the years when he might have been bewildered by the direction of his life, Edwards wrote what is considered to be his masterwork on God's sovereignty: *The Freedom of the Will*.

Who would want to be dismissed (we could say "fired") from a job? Jonathan Edwards, though, saw God's will in the situation and submitted to it. When confusing and frustrating things happen in our lives, let's consciously trust the providence of God. He has a plan, and He invites you to follow along.

*Lord, I trust You, even when my life goes differently than
I planned. Help me know that Your way is always best,
especially when I can't see it from my point of view.*

THE COST OF SERVING

"Rejoice and be glad, because great is your reward in heaven, for in the same way they persecuted the prophets who were before you."
MATTHEW 5:12 NIV

Pilot Nate Saint landed his plane on the remote Curaray River near a Waodani settlement. Surely, passenger Jim Elliot thought, the time had come for him and his four fellow missionaries to share the gospel with this remote and violent tribe.

The group stood on the shore, shouting Waodani words of greeting into the jungle. Soon, a Waodani party stepped out of the forest. Missionaries and natives exchanged a few words and gifts, and the tribesmen departed. Jim Elliot and his team stayed by the river and waited. Then a group of Waodani tribesmen arrived carrying spears. The missionaries tried to flee, but all five were killed.

If that's where the story ended, Jim Elliot's dreams would seem foolish. But not long afterward, one of the men who killed Jim and his friends accepted Christ. Mincaye even became a good friend to pilot Nate Saint's son.

Following Christ may not cost your life, but it always costs something—even if that's simply the disapproval of an antagonistic society. But if we truly believe Jesus, we know that any cost is worth a chance to share the gospel.

Lord, may I never hesitate to serve You.

FIGHTING THE GOOD FIGHT

*Fight the good fight of faith, lay hold on eternal life,
whereunto thou art also called, and hast professed
a good profession before many witnesses.*
1 TIMOTHY 6:12 KJV

William Booth, general of the Salvation Army, knew he was at war against Satan. As Ephesians 6:12 (KJV) says, "For we wrestle not against flesh and blood, but against principalities, against powers, against the rulers of the darkness of this world, against spiritual wickedness in high places."

Booth was a tenacious warrior. In one speech he said, "While women weep, as they do now, I'll fight; while little children go hungry, I'll fight; while men go to prison, in and out, in and out, as they do now, I'll fight—while there is a drunkard left, while there is a poor lost girl upon the streets, where there remains one dark soul without the light of God—I'll fight! I'll fight to the very end!"

It's easy to look at the darkness in the world and want to give up. Don't! We serve the God of light. Let Him fight through you, using every act of His love as a blow against the enemy.

*Lord, when I am discouraged by the fight, remind me
that You fight through me. And You will not lose!*

HOUR OF DECISION

"Suppose one of you wants to build a tower. Won't you first sit down and estimate the cost to see if you have enough money to complete it?"
LUKE 14:28 NIV

After the success of his Los Angeles crusade, Billy Graham was invited to preach around the world. Two men in Oregon believed that with his new popularity, Billy should launch another radio program. Unconvinced, Billy told them he'd consider the idea only if he could raise twenty-five thousand dollars before midnight that evening during his Portland crusade.

As the night wound down, twenty-*four* thousand dollars had been raised. But upon returning to his hotel room, Billy found two five-hundred-dollar checks waiting, both earmarked for the new radio ministry.

"Stunned, I bowed my head and said a silent prayer," Billy recorded in his book *Just As I Am*. "Emotion so overcame me that I could not think straight. Clearly, these funds had come from God."

God is never short on resources, but He keeps His funds in your pockets. Generous donors helped fund Billy Graham's *Hour of Decision* radio program, spreading the gospel on hundreds of stations. Are you using the money God's given you to further His kingdom?

Lord, all money is Yours. Help me to be faithful with the amount You've put in my care.

LEWIS' TRILEMMA

Jesus saith unto him, I am the way, the truth, and the life: no man cometh unto the Father, but by me.
JOHN 14:6 KJV

During World War II, C. S. Lewis was asked to give some BBC radio talks on Christianity. These talks became his book *Mere Christianity*. Lewis—a one-time atheist—used the opportunity to argue that either Jesus "was, and is, the Son of God, or else a madman or something worse."

To people who said Jesus was just a moral teacher, Lewis pointed to His claims to be one with the Father, alive before Moses, and able to forgive sins. "He would either be a lunatic—on the level with the man who says he is a poached egg—or else He would be the devil of hell. You must make your choice."

After looking at Jesus' claims, Lewis ruled out that He was either lunatic or devil—"consequently, however strange or terrifying or unlikely it may seem, I have to accept the view that He was and is God."

Who do you believe Jesus is? Are you treating Him simply as a great moral teacher? Or do you acknowledge Him (and His power) as the Son of God? Don't brush aside this essential issue.

Lord, You are the Son of God. Forgive me when I treat You as anything less.

ENCOURAGER IN PRISON

Blessed is the one who perseveres under trial because, having stood the test, that person will receive the crown of life that the Lord has promised to those who love him.
JAMES 1:12 NIV

In 1932, Eric Liddell became an ordained minister. Two years later, he was married, and Eric and his wife would have three daughters. The Liddells served as missionaries until 1937, when Japanese forces invaded China.

Four years later, the British government urged its subjects to leave China. Eric's wife and daughters moved to Canada. He stayed behind to tend to his flock.

After two more years, the Japanese army designated Eric an "enemy national." He was arrested and sent to a prison camp in Weihsien. Though the camp held eighteen hundred captives, it was slightly longer and wider than two football fields. Conditions were poor.

But Eric Liddell was remembered by fellow internees for his positive attitude and helpful activity. He preached, sang hymns, taught science to children, and even organized athletic events to encourage others.

How do you react when times get tough? It's easy to complain or withdraw. Take Eric Liddell for your example and start serving!

Father, help me to remain faithful to You and do Your work no matter what the circumstances of my life.

ON HARDSHIP

We are hard pressed on every side, but not crushed;
perplexed, but not in despair; persecuted, but not
abandoned; struck down, but not destroyed.
2 CORINTHIANS 4:8–9 NIV

On his initial expedition along the Zambezi River, David Livingstone became the first European to see the beautiful cataract he named Victoria Falls. Livingstone's belief that the Zambezi was key to opening Africa to new trade routes convinced the British government to fund a second expedition.

Livingstone set out in 1858, but his second trip was troubled. Falls and rapids along the river impeded the expedition's progress, and problems arose between Livingstone and his team. Four years into the journey, Livingstone returned to the coast where a steamboat, designed for exploring the inland Lake Malawi, arrived carrying his wife, Mary. She would soon die of malaria.

Through all the struggles, Livingstone refused to give up. "I am prepared to go anywhere," he said, "provided it be forward."

Our world can use more of that spirit, though Christians know the power behind it is their Lord. Like the apostle Paul in today's verse, we will face many hardships. But we don't face them alone. The God of mercy and power travels with us and will deliver each one of us safely where He wants us to be.

Lord, when I am hard pressed, keep me from despair.

MARRIED PRIEST

*He who finds a wife finds what is good
and receives favor from the LORD.*
PROVERBS 18:22 NIV

"Suddenly, and while I was occupied with far different thoughts, the Lord has plunged me into marriage." So wrote Martin Luther about his unexpected relationship with Katharina von Bora, a former nun.

Katharina was one of twelve nuns who appealed to Luther for help in escaping a Cistercian monastery. Luther sent a fish cart, and the nuns were smuggled out amid a load of herring barrels.

Eleven of the women found husbands quickly. Twenty-six-year-old Katharina had suitors but felt drawn to the helpful former monk, fifteen years her senior. He had ruled out marriage due to his pending arrest on heresy charges, but God knew that for Luther's work to continue, he needed a strong partner.

Marriage was a game changer for the burgeoning Reformation, as clergymen found wives who supported their ministries. Marriage is always a game changer, because it helps us all see Christ as a caring husband who woos His bride, the church. If you are a Christian—whether you're married or not—you are engaged to Jesus Christ. Are you fully invested in this relationship that will last for eternity?

*Lord, may I love You more each day, seeking
ways to enjoy our relationship more fully.*

CHICAGO EVANGELIZATION SOCIETY

> *Then he said to his disciples, "The harvest is plentiful*
> *but the workers are few. Ask the Lord of the harvest,*
> *therefore, to send out workers into his harvest field."*
> MATTHEW 9:37–38 NIV

Dwight L. Moody was a key figure of nineteenth-century Christianity. But he's influential even in the twenty-first century because of Emma Dryer.

She was a schoolteacher in Chicago, Moody's adopted hometown. In 1870, D. L. convinced Emma to apply her skills at his church. After the Great Chicago Fire destroyed the church building and Moody went abroad, Emma Dryer stepped into the gap, developing a program of Bible study, teaching, and home visitation for young women.

Dryer prayed Moody would come back to Chicago and open a school where men and women could be equipped to spread the gospel. Her prayers were answered: in 1886, the Chicago Evangelization Society (today, the Moody Bible Institute) was founded.

As an evangelist, D. L. Moody reached thousands for Christ— but as an organization, the Moody Bible Institute has trained thousands to reach countless thousands more. Whether or not you've had specialized training, God calls you to be part of the soul-winning effort. The fields are still waiting for faithful workers.

Lord, prepare me to be a faithful harvester for You.

HEAVENLY PRIORITIES

*"You must love the LORD your God with all your heart,
all your soul, all your mind, and all your strength."*
MARK 12:30 NLT

When Samuel Morris reached New York City, God miraculously led him to Stephen Merritt. This man, who knew the missionary who'd led Samuel to the Lord, took the former African prince under his wing. Merritt lined up financial donors and wrote to Taylor University urging Samuel's acceptance as a student.

One day, Merritt showed the young man around New York, pointing out places of interest. Samuel asked if Merritt had ever prayed in his carriage, then suggested they pray together. Merritt recalled, "He told the Holy Spirit he had come from Africa to talk to me about Him, and I talked about everything else, and wanted to show him the church, the city, and the people, when he was so desirous of hearing and knowing about Him, and he asked Him if He would take out of my heart things, and so fill me with Himself that I would never write, or preach, or talk only of Him."

Stephen Merritt was a committed Christian who helped Samuel Morris tremendously—but was convicted by his young friend's single-minded devotion. It's easy to be distracted by this world. If you find yourself in Stephen Merritt's place today, ask God to give you His heavenly priorities.

*Lord, take away my love of this world
and replace it with Yourself.*

FINANCIAL TRANSPARENCY

*Therefore each of you must put off falsehood
and speak truthfully to your neighbor, for
we are all members of one body.*
EPHESIANS 4:25 NIV

At age sixteen, George Müller spent time in prison for unpaid hotel bills. He was only released when his father paid his debt.

Four years later, while enrolled at Halle University to study theology, George arranged a trip to Switzerland with friends who entrusted him with their finances. They didn't realize George had charged them all more so he didn't have to pay as much. Later that year, though, Müller was saved—and his behavior started to change.

Years later, when George was overseeing the care of thousands of orphans by unsolicited donations, he meticulously worked to prevent anyone from cheating donors out of their money. Every gift was issued a receipt, whether the donation was a few pennies, thousands of dollars, or a spoon.

In order for others to see the financial miracles at Müller's orphanages, they needed to trust the donation accounting was accurate. Our trust in God should always result in greater transparency with the world. How are you presenting yourself to those around you?

*Lord, where I've been false, let me speak
truthfully. Give me courage to live transparently
in this world, so others can see You clearly.*

FINDING GOD IN THE HAPHAZARD

*Thou wilt keep him in perfect peace, whose mind
is stayed on thee: because he trusteth in thee.*
ISAIAH 26:3 KJV

Oswald Chambers, the man behind the classic devotional *My Utmost for His Highest,* was a preacher, evangelist, and military chaplain. Though teaching was always an aspect of his ministry, he actually ran a school in London for about five years.

And Chambers didn't just oversee the school, he built it from scratch. . .in about a month.

Having been part of small, ministry-focused colleges in Dunoon, Scotland, and Cincinnati, Ohio, Chambers dreamed of starting his own. The organization he'd been serving with, the League of Prayer, rented an excellent building and turned him loose. The Bible Training College was up and running in weeks, purely by faith.

"God's order comes to us in the haphazard," Chambers taught. "We try to plan our ways and work things out for ourselves, but they go wrong because there are more facts than we know; if we just go on with the days as they come, we find that God's order comes to us in that apparently haphazard way."

We'll never know everything about this life, but we serve a God who does. Trust Him to guide you, and provide peace along the way.

---

*Lord, I trust You with my future.
Thank You for the peace You offer.*

ABOLITIONIST PRIEST

> *For if we sin wilfully after that we have*
> *received the knowledge of the truth, there*
> *remaineth no more sacrifice for sins.*
> HEBREWS 10:26 KJV

For nine years after poor health forced him from the sea, John Newton studied to become a minister. In 1764, he was appointed an Anglican priest in Olney.

His participation in the slave trade behind him, John Newton could have ignored this history to focus on his new role. Instead, when the abolition cause reached Parliament in the 1780s, Newton wrote and distributed *Thoughts Upon the African Slave Trade*.

"I hope it will always be a subject of humiliating reflection to me that I was once an active instrument in a business at which my heart now shudders," he wrote. "Perhaps what I have said of myself may be applicable to the nation at large. The slave trade was always unjustifiable; but inattention and interest prevented for a time the evil from being perceived. It is otherwise at present."

Newton lived to see Britain outlaw the slave trade in 1807.

Our poor choices, even ones we deliberately pursued for years, need not determine our legacy. It's never too late to do the right thing. Who knows how God will use your mistakes to bring Himself glory?

> *Lord, give me the courage to change.*
> *Use all of my choices for Your glory.*

Luis Palau

A FRIENDLY DIALOGUE

> *And I give unto them eternal life; and they shall never perish, neither shall any man pluck them out of my hand.*
> JOHN 10:28 KJV

In 2008, Luis Palau published a book with Zhao Qizheng, minister of information for the People's Republic of China. *A Friendly Dialogue Between an Atheist and a Christian* was a transcript of recorded dialogs held in 2005.

During one meeting, Palau gave Qizheng a Bible inscribed with John 10:28. In an interview with The Christian Post, Luis said:

"It's not in the book but I always tell the story of my father dying. . . . He died knowing he was going to heaven, that he had the assurance of eternal life. He died clapping and singing a song about heaven and quoting Philippians 1: 'I'm going to be with Jesus which is better by far.' "

With his own mother dying, Qizheng was inspired. "To me," he said, "his view of eternity was so, so moving that his father was at peace, he was singing, he was clapping, he knew where he was going."

For Christians, there is no despair in death. God has made a way for us to be with Him, forever. It's a truth that even appeals to atheists.

Lord, thank You for the assurance of my salvation!

GUARDIAN OF THE CHURCH

*We have different gifts, according to the grace
given to each of us. If your gift is prophesying,
then prophesy in accordance with your faith; it if is
serving, then serve; if it is teaching, then teach.*
ROMANS 12:6–7 NIV

When Valerius, the bishop of Hippo died, Augustine stepped in to fill the void. He was quickly confronted with challenges in the church. Augustine fought Manichaeism, a mixture of Christianity and Persian religion, as well as Donatism, a heresy that was splitting the church in Africa. His education and training—especially in philosophy and rhetoric—allowed him to blunt the impact of these harmful beliefs.

When he became a Christian, Augustine had hoped to maintain a simple lifestyle, away from the spotlight. But God had other plans. A brilliant scholar, now deeply immersed in scripture, he could use his training in debate to stand up for truth. God used Augustine's gifts to keep the church together, even after the fall of Rome.

Our gifts may differ, widely, from Augustine's. But if you enjoy singing on the worship team, do that to your fullest capability. Or if you love to shovel snow or mow grass for widows, do that to God's glory. All of our gifts are designed to benefit our Lord's body, the church.

*Lord, help me to use the gifts You have
given me to bring glory to Your name.*

TOO MUCH FLESH

But God showed his great love for us by sending
Christ to die for us while we were still sinners.
ROMANS 5:8 NLT

Charles Spurgeon, who died in 1892, was (and still is) known for his preaching. In his time, he was also recognized for his large frame and his wit.

A man once wanted to transfer membership to Spurgeon's church. The famed pastor wrote to the other church, asking if there was anything in the man's character that would prevent membership.

"The reply they sent was laconic, but not particularly lucid," Spurgeon recalled. " 'The man has too much of the flesh.' When he called to hear the result of his application, I sent for a yard or two of string, and asked one of our friends to take my measure, and then to take his. As I found that I had much more 'flesh' than he had, and as his former associates had nothing else to allege against him, I proposed him for church membership, and he was in due course accepted."

Charles Spurgeon was willing to accept a man in spite of his past—just like God accepts each of us when we are born again. We are no longer measured by our sins, but by Jesus Christ's sacrifice. Why not offer a prayer of thanks for that right now?

Lord, You don't judge me for my past.
May I extend grace as freely to others.

GENEROUS REVIVALIST

You will be enriched in every way so that you can be
generous on every occasion, and through us your
generosity will result in thanksgiving to God.
2 CORINTHIANS 9:11 NIV

There is no doubt that Billy Sunday made significant money as a traveling evangelist. By some estimates, he and his wife, Helen, brought in more than a million dollars between 1908 and 1920. Government statistics for 1920 indicate the average income per tax return was less than thirty-three hundred dollars.

Sunday's income may sound exorbitant, and we might quickly think of the Bible's warnings about "the love of money" (1 Timothy 6:10). But there's another side of the equation. The Sundays were incredibly generous with the money they received.

After a Chicago revival, Billy Sunday gave fifty-eight thousand dollars to the Pacific Garden Mission, the organization that helped bring him to the faith. He and his wife donated over one hundred and twenty thousand dollars to charities supporting soldiers in the Great War (World War I). And Sunday's mentor reported he could not remember a time when Billy had not offered him financial help.

Money itself is not evil, it's a tool for good. "A generous person will prosper," (Proverbs 11:25 NIV).

Father, show me how I can be generous with
my resources and bring glory to Your name.

CHINA INLAND MISSION

*So let us come boldly to the throne of our gracious
God. There we will receive his mercy, and we will
find grace to help us when we need it most.*
HEBREWS 4:16 NLT

When Hudson Taylor returned from his sabbatical on the southern shores of England, he had a sense of peace and a new idea: the China Inland Mission. This organization would be distinctly different from all other missionary organizations.

CIM would not guarantee salaries, nor could their missionaries ask for money—they had to rely on God's provision. Instead of donning their English attire, they were to dress like the people they encountered in the field. In under a year, Hudson Taylor, his family, and twenty-one missionaries were ready to serve the Lord in China.

But funds were not the only thing Hudson Taylor prayed for. According to *Christian History* magazine, "In 1881, he asked God for another 70 missionaries by the close of 1884: he got 76. In late 1886, Taylor prayed for another 100 within a year: by November 1887, he announced 102 candidates had been accepted for service."

Hudson Taylor believed that God would take care of His people. What are your needs today? Pray. The same God that answered Hudson Taylor listens to you.

Father, thank You for hearing my prayers today.

William Tyndale

BETRAYAL IN ANTWERP

Faithful are the wounds of a friend;
but the kisses of an enemy are deceitful.
PROVERBS 27:6 KJV

William Tyndale, pioneer of English Bible translation, met his downfall when he crossed paths with a certain Henry Phillips.

Tall and handsome, Phillips came from an influential English family. But he gambled away his money and found himself stranded in Antwerp. Rumor was that Tyndale was in the city, working on his English Bible. An enemy of Tyndale's work—it's unclear exactly who it was—engaged Phillips to find the translator.

With his natural charm, Phillips quickly infiltrated the English merchant scene and found Tyndale staying among them. Phillips befriended Tyndale easily, then waited for the right moment to lure him into a trap. When the time came, Phillips led Tyndale to the authorities—shortly after "borrowing" money from him!

God calls us to love everyone. But He also warns us to choose our friends carefully. Are your friends guiding you into a greater relationship with God? Or are they leading you toward a fall?

Lord, give me wisdom in choosing my friends.
May I spend time with those people who point me
toward You—and may I do the same for them.

DON'T STOP DOING GOOD

*Being confident of this, that he who began
a good work in you will carry it on to
completion until the day of Christ Jesus.*
PHILIPPIANS 1:6 NIV

For a time, John Wesley helped preach to George Whitefield's overflow crowds. The two men would ultimately part ways over the issue of predestination, but the experience of reaching the masses for Christ lit a fire that would burn for the rest of Wesley's life.

He began to organize converts into "societies," small groups of individuals who met in homes to pray, read the Bible, and discuss their spiritual struggles. Once a society grew too large, Wesley would start another one. Each was led by a "class leader."

The societies grew rapidly, and Wesley developed the structure of a new organization. Critics arose to complain that Wesley was working around the official Church of England, and some opponents even resorted to violence. But Wesley kept at it, and his work eventually became the Methodist church, with members and congregations around the world.

Not every spiritual endeavor grows so dramatically. But if God has called you to a ministry, He will do His work through it. Your job is simply to remain faithful.

*Father, provide me strength to continue
to reach others for Jesus.*

NOT ALWAYS POPULAR

*To one who listens, valid criticism is like a
gold earring or other gold jewelry.*
PROVERBS 25:12 NLT

Though he was well known, George Whitefield was not always popular.

One woman tried to attack him with scissors and a pistol before finally using her teeth. Other people threw stones and dead cats at him. One man climbed a tree to urinate on Whitefield as he passed underneath. Another bludgeoned the evangelist with a brass-tipped cane. After each attack, Whitefield kept preaching.

He was known for being provocative in the pulpit. Whitefield once said, "It is a poor sermon that gives no offense; that neither makes the hearer displeased with himself nor with the preacher."

Have you ever had a sermon affect you like that? How did you react? If the preaching of God's Word elicits an emotional reaction, first ask yourself why—and then ask God to keep working in you.

(And, we might add, if you've *never* heard a sermon that challenged you, maybe it's time to visit another church.)

*Lord, keep me from growing angry
when I should be growing wise.*

William Wilberforce

THE CLAPHAM SECT

As iron sharpens iron, so one person sharpens another.
PROVERBS 27:17 NIV

In 1790 William Wilberforce moved to Clapham, England, joining a group of Christians called the Clapham Sect. This group included several members of Parliament and other prominent Christians in this area of London. Their main concern was to integrate Christian ideals into business and government.

The Clapham Sect fought for the abolition of slaves, and supported missionaries, schools for children, and Bible societies. Members even sought to improve prison conditions. Though they were all wealthy and prominent individuals, the Clapham Sect consciously looked beyond themselves.

Wilberforce would write in 1797, "Selfishness is one of the principal fruits of the corruption of human nature; and it is obvious that selfishness disposes us to overrate our good qualities, and to overlook or extenuate our defects." Living in community kept these Christians accountable to one another as they pursued what God had laid on their hearts.

Do you have a small group of Christians who speaks into your life? If not, seek some out. As iron sharpens iron, the Proverb says, so one person sharpens another.

---

*Lord, thank You for the believers who have influenced
my life. Please continue to bring me the right
people at the right time in my Christian walk.*

THE WYCLIFFE BIBLE

For the word of God is alive and active. Sharper than any double-edged sword, it penetrates even to dividing soul and spirit, joints and marrow; it judges the thoughts and attitudes of the heart.
HEBREWS 4:12 NIV

In the fourteenth century, the Bible was walled off from most people. It was copied in Latin and kept in the hands of Catholic church leadership. Common people only had access to what the church chose to reveal.

In his third book, *On the Truth of Sacred Scripture*, John Wycliffe declared it was time for everyone to have access to scripture. The church disagreed, but Wycliffe began translating God's Word into English anyway, knowing full well this "heresy" was punishable by death.

According to a church leader of the time, "By this translation, the scriptures have become vulgar, and they are more available to laymen, and even to women who can read, than they were to learned scholars, who have a high intelligence. So the pearl of the gospel is scattered and trodden underfoot by swine."

In the twenty-first century, we have access to dozens of English Bible translations. The important question for us is this: Do we take advantage of this incredible wealth of information? Never forget that earlier believers watered the seeds of our harvest with their own blood.

Father, create in me a deep love for scripture.

Dietrich Bonhoeffer

FAITHFUL TO THE END

*Everyone who competes in the games goes into strict
training. They do it to get a crown that will not last,
but we do it to get a crown that will last forever.*
1 CORINTHIANS 9:25 NIV

Amid all the insanity of Nazi Germany, Dietrich Bonhoeffer continued to serve and follow God. But, it seemed, evil would win as he was arrested for aiding Jews, imprisoned for two years as a resister, and ultimately executed at the Flossenbürg extermination camp.

Years later, an eyewitness to his hanging would write, "I saw pastor Bonhoeffer, before taking off his prison garb, kneeling on the floor praying fervently to his God. I was most deeply moved by the way this lovable man prayed, so devout and so certain that God heard his prayer." After another prayer, Bonhoeffer mounted the steps to the gallows and calmly entered eternity.

Even as Dietrich Bonhoeffer took his final steps, people were watching. Thankfully, we have record of a brave man of faith who finished well.

People are watching all of us, in our reactions to the big, scary events of life but also the daily little joys and sorrows. How does your faith look to outsiders? Does it need some "strict training" to be more successful?

*Father, may I be an example—in every
situation—that brings glory to Your name.*

MAKE SEEING EYES BLIND

*So we say with confidence, "The Lord is my helper;
I will not be afraid. What can mere mortals do to me?"*
HEBREWS 13:6 NIV

Brother Andrew smuggled Bibles into countries that had been closed to Christianity for decades. His travels took him from eastern Europe to the Middle East to China. He experienced many close calls with authorities.

Because these encounters with hostile authorities were so common, Brother Andrew developed a prayer to recite when he ran into trouble: "Lord, in my luggage I have scripture I want to take to your children. When you were on earth, You made blind eyes see. Now, I pray, make seeing eyes blind. Do not let the guards see those things You do not want them to see."

God was pleased to answer this prayer of Brother Andrew, who continued his daring ministry for years through the organization Open Doors.

Few of us will face the dangers that Brother Andrew did, but we all encounter opportunities to share the gospel. They may be around the world or just around the corner—but wherever they are, God will equip you for the work. Ask for His help to have the boldness of Brother Andrew.

*Father, give me perseverance to bear
the message of hope in Jesus.*

FINDING PEACE

Precious in the sight of the LORD is the death of his saints.
PSALM 116:15 KJV

After the publication of *The Pilgrim's Progress*, John Bunyan became a sought-after preacher. He was also known as a peacemaker. On his way to London in 1688, Bunyan took a detour to Reading to resolve a disagreement between a father and son.

After a successful reunion, Bunyan resumed his trip to London through inclement weather. He fell ill on the way, and ten days later he died.

John Bunyan's writing has influenced notable authors like Charles Dickens, Mark Twain, Louisa May Alcott, and C. S. Lewis. . .but was that what made him a great Christian? No—John Bunyan was great for the same reason you are—because of Jesus Christ.

If you worry whether things you say or do remove God's love from you, set that burden down. God loves us because His Son died to save our souls—not because of anything we've done. Once we understand that, we can truly live for Him like John Bunyan did, finding peace with God ourselves and helping others to find it too.

Lord, thank You for loving me. Use me to
bring Your love and peace to others.

TIRELESS CHAMPION OF CHRIST

*Never be lacking in zeal, but keep your
spiritual fervor, serving the Lord.*
ROMANS 12:11 NIV

John Calvin's protest against the dominant Catholic church (from which we get the term *protestant*) led him to write books, including the influential *Institutes of the Christian Religion*. Often on the run from unhappy church leaders, he eventually settled in Geneva where he attempted to set up a theocratic society—one based on biblical principles. Though some today question the wisdom and results of that attempt, few doubt the fervor that drove it.

Calvin was tireless in teaching, writing, and counseling to promote the gospel of Christ. When he was ill, he taught from his bed. When his legs failed him, he was carried to the church to preach. When doctors kept him out of the winter air, he taught lessons in his home. To the friends who urged him to slow down, Calvin responded, "What? Would you have the Lord find me idle when he comes?"

There is a balance to find in Christian work. Jesus got away, and urged His disciples to do the same, for quiet and rest (Mark 6:31). And yet He also commanded us to work before the night comes (John 9:4). John Calvin worked tirelessly. How hard are we working for Christ's kingdom?

*Father, please give me the strength to
do Your work like John Calvin did.*

COMMISSION FULFILLED

> *Then Jesus came to them and said, "All authority in heaven and on earth has been given to me. Therefore go and make disciples of all nations, baptizing them in the name of the Father and of the Son and of the Holy Spirit."*
> MATTHEW 28:18–19 NIV

William Carey died in the mission field after serving for forty-one consecutive years. Imagine—more than four decades without a furlough, in the service of Jesus Christ. That's impressive dedication. But in a nation of millions, Carey is said to have led only about seven hundred people to the Christian faith. Was he a success?

Before you answer, consider that William Carey helped translate the entire Bible into India's six major languages and parts of scripture into many others. His actions ignited missions work worldwide and influenced many prominent missionaries of the nineteenth century. These facts far outweigh the number of converts Carey produced.

Like many Bible characters, William Carey did not live to see what his faithfulness inspired. He simply obeyed and left the results to God.

How about you? Are you focused on building your own legacy? Or are you serving the cause of Christ focused solely on making *His* name great?

> *Father, may I be focused on Your legacy, not my own. Use my life to glorify You.*

SUCCESS REDEFINED

*"What good will it be for someone to gain the
whole world, yet forfeit their soul? Or what can
anyone give in exchange for their soul?"*
MATTHEW 16:26 NIV

Before he died in 1943, George Washington Carver was awarded the highest honor of the National Association for the Advancement of Colored People, honorary doctorates from Simpson College and Selma University, and a fellowship from the Royal Society of Arts in Great Britain. Since his death, Carver's name has been memorialized in schools, parks, and even a US Navy submarine.

Though well known in both life and death, Carver did not count fame as evidence of success. He said, "It is not the style of clothes one wears, neither the kind of automobiles one drives, nor the amount of money one has in the bank that counts. These mean nothing. It is simple service that measures success."

The Bible agrees: "Whoever wants to become great among you must be your servant, and whoever wants to be first must be slave of all. For even the Son of Man did not come to be served, but to serve, and to give his life as a ransom for many" (Mark 10:43–45 NIV).

Want to be great? Start serving! It's never too late to start working toward true success.

*Lord, I don't need fame to be successful.
Give me a servant's heart instead.*

DEFENDER OF THE OPPRESSED

> *Learn to do right; seek justice. Defend*
> *the oppressed. Take up the cause of the*
> *fatherless; plead the case of the widow.*
> ISAIAH 1:17 NIV

Frederick Douglass left an astounding legacy. He had lectured thousands of times, mainly focusing on equal rights for African Americans and women. He wrote five books, started two newspapers, advised presidents, and was the first African American to hold a high US government office, as minister to Haiti.

Douglass burned with passion for oppressed people, going to great lengths, in spite of great opposition, to speak out for those without a voice. Throughout his seventy-seven years, he worked tirelessly, doing all in his power to create change where he saw culture in conflict with the gospel.

There's a simpler way to say that, as Galatians 6:2 (NIV) puts it: "Carry each other's burdens, and in this way you will fulfill the law of Christ."

The world is full of trouble, and trying to make positive change can be overwhelming. But you can change one person's world with a well-timed word of encouragement or offer of help. Whose burden can you help carry today?

Lord, call my attention to the injustice around me,
and help me to carry another person's burden.

LEGACY OF FAITH

He must increase, but I must decrease.
JOHN 3:30 KJV

Jonathan Edwards was a pastor, theologian, and missionary whose writings continue to influence whole generations. But he was even more than that.

Edwards was the father of eleven children. His numerous descendants would go on to be ministers, professors, and political leaders, including a US vice president (Aaron Burr). Though Jonathan Edwards set a good example for his family to follow, he did not want them to see him as anything other than a humble man in need of a Savior.

"A truly humble man is sensible of his natural distance from God," he wrote, "of his dependence on Him; of the insufficiency of his own power and wisdom; and that it is by God's power that he is upheld and provided for, and that he needs God's wisdom to lead and guide him, and His might to enable him to do what he ought to do for Him."

If the legacy you hope to leave inspires people to look at your life instead of God, it will not last. Live so people will see God in you and follow Him.

Lord, make me less, so people can see You more.

GIVING IT ALL

> *"For whoever wants to save their life will lose it,*
> *but whoever loses their life for me will find it."*
> MATTHEW 16:25 NIV

Jim Elliot knew Jesus at age six and met the Lord before his thirtieth birthday. His goal in life was to share Christ with others, but he often felt frustrated that he saw no fruit. Elliot wrote in his journal, "No fruit yet. Why is it that I'm so unproductive? I cannot recall leading more than one or two into the kingdom. Surely this is not the manifestation of the power of the Resurrection. I feel as Rachel, 'Give me children, or else I die.' "

When Jim Elliot and his four fellow missionaries were killed in Ecuador, it laid the foundation for Jesus to be shared with the entire world. Through his death, Jim was able to reach thousands of people for Christ—including the violent Waodoni people who had taken his life. His life and mission have been depicted in numerous books and films.

We never know what the cost of serving Christ might be. But we know for sure what we gain—eternal life through the power of Jesus' resurrection.

Father, may I never count the cost of following You.

DOER OF THE WORD

*But be ye doers of the word, and not hearers
only, deceiving your own selves.*
JAMES 1:22 KJV

The primary mission of William Booth's Salvation Army has always been to win people to Christ. But Booth knew that people worried about getting their next meal aren't really thinking about their souls.

Today, the Salvation Army offers assistance in more than one hundred countries around the world. Through homeless shelters, charity shops, humanitarian-crisis and natural-disaster relief, the organization seeks to be the hands and feet of Jesus to all people, regardless of their beliefs.

The needy may be brought in physically by food, clothing, or shelter, but they are won over spiritually through prayer. Clever arguments for Christianity can't hold a candle to meeting a person's needs and praying for them. As Booth once said, "Argument never opened the eyes of the blind. Do not argue, but pray."

When was the last time you helped someone in need? When was the last time you prayed a person would come to know Christ? Take a moment right now to talk with God about people's souls and their practical needs you can meet.

*Lord, the opportunities to help others are there. Give me
the eyes to see them and the will to meet them today.*

ON CIVIL RIGHTS

> *Jew and Gentile are the same in this respect.*
> *They have the same Lord, who gives*
> *generously to all who call on him.*
> ROMANS 10:12 NLT

Although Billy Graham's earliest crusades were segregated, by the 1950s he had removed the racial barriers within his audience. Graham told volunteers to keep the barriers down "or you can go on and have the revival without me."

In 1957, Billy incorporated African Americans into his crusades, inviting Dr. Martin Luther King Jr. to speak at a revival in New York City. The two became close friends. King even invited Billy to call him by his nickname, "Mike."

Billy Graham was in Australia when King was murdered in 1968. Upon hearing the news, Graham said, "I was almost in a state of shock. Not only was I losing a friend through a vicious and senseless killing, but America was losing a social leader and a prophet, and I felt his death would be one of the greatest tragedies in our history."

The gospel is not for one group of people, but for all. Don't allow skin color, ethnicity, or any other physical feature to keep you from welcoming another person. We're all created in God's image—and equally needy before Jesus' cross.

Lord, give me Your perspective. Help me love
all people, regardless of background.

MARRIAGE WITH JOY

And now these three remain: faith, hope and
love. But the greatest of these is love.
1 CORINTHIANS 13:13 NIV

In his later years, C. S. Lewis (or "Jack" as he was called) unexpectedly fell in love with American writer and divorcée Joy Davidman.

"For Jack the attraction was at first undoubtedly intellectual," wrote Jack's brother, Warren. "Joy was the only woman whom he had met (although his letters show, he had known with great affection many able women) who had a brain which matched his own in suppleness, in width of interest, and in analytical grasp, and above all in humour and a sense of fun."

In order to stay in England, Joy married Jack in a civil ceremony in 1956. In 1957, their relationship shifted toward heartfelt love and they spoke Christian vows in the hospital where Joy was being treated for terminal cancer. After a temporary recovery, she passed away in 1960.

Both in Lewis' marriage and in his spiritual life, love grew out of intellectual intrigue. When it comes to God's love, are you in the intellectual phase or do you have a heartfelt love? Pray that God would continuously move you from loving knowledge about Him to knowing love with Him.

Lord, I want to know You. . .but I
need to love You even more.

RADIANT GODLINESS

That is why, for Christ's sake, I delight in weaknesses,
in insults, in hardships, in persecutions, in difficulties.
For when I am weak, then I am strong.
2 CORINTHIANS 12:10 NIV

As a Japanese prisoner of war in China, Eric Liddell still cared for the spiritual and physical well-being of those around him. David Mitchell, a child interned in the Weihsien camp, vividly remembered Eric and how he served. "None of us will ever forget this man who was totally committed to putting God first," Mitchell wrote, "a man whose humble life combined muscular Christianity with radiant godliness."

Sadly, only six months before the camp was liberated by American troops in August 1945, Eric Liddell died of a brain tumor. He was forty-three years old.

Regardless of his circumstances, Eric Liddell did his best to point others toward Jesus. Whether he was being cheered for his Olympic achievements or he was imprisoned away from his family, Liddell shined as a humble servant of Christ.

What would people say about you? Can your life be said to combine "muscular Christianity and radiant godliness"?

Lord, may others see Jesus Christ reflected
in all my words and actions.

ABOLITIONIST EXPLORER

> *"Kidnappers must be put to death, whether they are caught in possession of their victims or have already sold them as slaves."*
> Exodus 21:16 NLT

After his dreadful second expedition to Africa (1858–64), David Livingstone was recalled to England. Within two years, he was going back to find the source of the Nile River.

That was a subject of great curiosity in Europe, but Livingstone had other reasons for the journey. "If the good Lord permits me to put a stop to the enormous evils of the inland slave trade," he said, "I shall not grudge my hunger and toils. I shall bless His name with all my heart. The Nile sources are valuable to me only as a means of enabling me to open my mouth with power among men."

Livingstone never returned from his expedition. Beset by trials, he was forced to accept aid from the very slave traders he was trying to stop. But in the end, his eyewitness reports on this "immense evil" stirred up public sentiment for its abolition.

Not everyone is a crusader like David Livingstone. But we each live in a world of trouble and have a certain amount of influence to exert. What societal issues grieve you most? What can you do to fight the "enormous evils" of today's world?

Lord, may I use the gifts You've given me to fight the evils of this day.

A MIGHTY FORTRESS IS OUR GOD

God is our refuge and strength,
a very present help in trouble.
PSALM 46:1 KJV

Not only is Martin Luther credited with launching the Reformation, he is responsible for the rallying song that inspired its followers. Luther was a prolific hymn writer, the most famous of which is Ein' feste Burg ist unser Gott ("A Mighty Fortress Is Our God").

It is said that Luther sang this hymn as he walked toward judgment at the Holy Roman Empire's Diet of Worms in 1521. It's been played when soldiers march off to war. It's been adapted by Johann Sebastian Bach, Felix Mendelssohn, and Richard Wagner, among others.

Why has this hymn inspired people for five centuries? The music and message both resound with strength. They reassure us that no matter how strong evil may seem, it is nothing compared to the strength of God. This world, the spiritual battles that rage around us, and our own bodies will pass away, but "God's truth abideth still, His kingdom is forever."

As you face earthly hardship, remember the eternal perspective. Our God is omnipotent. When we find our identity in His love, we are held safe regardless of the conflict around us.

Lord, You are my security. Help me remember
You've already won the battle.

DEALING WITH DISRUPTION

*For whosoever shall call upon the name
of the Lord shall be saved.*
ROMANS 10:13 KJV

In 1893, Chicago hosted the World's Columbian Exposition, a fair celebrating the four hundredth anniversary of Europeans' arrival in the New World. Replicas of the *Niña*, the *Pinta*, and the *Santa María* sailed across the Atlantic for the occasion. New products like Cream of Wheat, Juicy Fruit Gum, and the brownie were displayed for the first time.

While some church leaders were angry that the fair would be open on Sundays, D. L. Moody saw opportunity. His goal was simple: "Let us open so many preaching places and present the gospel so attractively that people will want to come and hear it."

For months, Moody and his church prepared sites across the city where the gospel could be preached to the millions who would attend the fair. He even got permission to use a giant circus tent for morning services before the afternoon and evening shows. The church services actually outdrew the circus!

Though firm in his theology, Moody was adaptable in his methods. He saw the exposition as an opportunity for God to change lives. We can take the same attitude toward the new and unusual aspects of our culture. Just dedicate the disruptions to the Lord and watch Him work!

*Lord, help me see opportunities when I
would normally see disruption.*

INFLUENTIAL STUDENT

*Commit to the LORD whatever you do,
and he will establish your plans.*
PROVERBS 16:3 NIV

Thanks to the donations of others, in 1891 a former African prince became a student at Taylor University. Now known as Samuel Morris, the young man requested the dorm room no one else wanted. In a short time, he profoundly changed the campus by his presence.

Two years later, Morris was dead. College president Thaddeus Reade wrote, "Long before we apprehended that his sickness was serious he told us that he had heard his Master call and he must go. When I spoke to him of the work he had so fondly hoped to do among his people, he would answer, 'Others can do it better. It is not my work, it is Christ's work; He must choose His own workers.' "

At the young man's memorial service, a student stood up to say he sensed God telling him to work with Samuel's Kru tribe. He was followed by two other students who felt the same way.

God will choose His own workers. If He has placed a burden on your heart, follow that lead. If He has blocked you from a work you thought you should do, accept His guidance. Commit whatever you do to Him, and He will establish your plans.

Lord, reveal Your work to me so I can follow Your lead.

SHARE WHAT GOD HAS DONE

Then I heard the voice of the Lord saying,
"Whom shall I send? And who will go for
us?" And I said, "Here am I. Send me!"
ISAIAH 6:8 NIV

George Müller provided housing for more than 10,000 English orphans. He established 117 schools through which he gave some 120,000 students a Christian education. But his work went beyond serving needy youth.

When Müller turned seventy, he became a missionary. For the next seventeen years he traveled two hundred thousand miles to address more than three million people in forty-two countries. "The more I am in a position to be tried in faith with reference to my body, my family, my service for the Lord, my business," Müller said, "the more shall I have the opportunity of seeing God's help and deliverance; and every fresh instance, in which He helps and delivers me, will tend towards the increase of my faith."

Through his powerful and persistent prayer, George Müller had received everything he needed for his long and effective ministry. And he told people about it so they would trust God too.

Never keep God's faithfulness to yourself. Share what the Lord has done for you! Your family and friends will be encouraged to hear how He provides.

Father, I remember how You have showed up in my life.
Help me share Your faithfulness with someone today!

SPEND AND BE SPENT

I will very gladly spend and be spent for you.
2 CORINTHIANS 12:15 KJV

Oswald Chambers thought his London-based Bible Training College (BTC) was "the Gate of Heaven." With his wife, Biddy, he oversaw a ministry preparation program in a large, apartment-style building that allowed the leaders and two dozen students to live and serve together.

But as the British Empire entered the Great War—now called World War I—Chambers felt an unbearable urge to serve the soldiers. When God opened a door through the YMCA, the now-chaplain phased out his beloved school. For the next two years, until his shocking death following an appendectomy, Chambers would live like the apostle Paul, spending and being spent for his flock.

In the Egyptian desert, soldiers from Australia, New Zealand, and the home island recalled Chambers' tireless work on their behalf. One fellow minister described him as "always busy but never flurried." Another recalled, "I see him in the heat of the day, denying himself the rest that was his due, coming out to a canvas hospital on a visit to someone laid aside."

The Proverbs teach that a generous man will himself be refreshed (11:25). It isn't easy to spend and be spent for others—but God promises to repay whatever we give up for Him.

Lord, help me to spend and be spent for others.

AMAZING GRACE

"And as if this were not enough in your sight, my God, you have spoken about the future of the house of your servant. You, LORD God, have looked on me as though I were the most exalted of men."
1 CHRONICLES 17:17 NIV

The Anglican church of Olney, England, had a former slave ship captain as its pastor. John Newton regularly admitted his failings, and the congregation loved him.

One of the church members, William Cowper, had experienced his own strange path to salvation. He was one of the most admired poets of his day but had suffered from bouts of insanity before coming to Christ.

Cowper began collaborating with Newton on weekly songs to accompany the sermons. *Olney Hymns*, a collection of their work together, was published in 1779 and included a piece called "Faith's Review and Expectation"—better known as "Amazing Grace (How Sweet the Sound)."

The poem was Newton's autobiography, and though it fell into relative obscurity in England, it was embraced as a gospel hymn in the American South. Today, it is one of the most recognizable songs on the planet.

Even more amazing than the song's origin is the grace it proclaims. God's forgiveness is still available for anyone who asks. Are you living in the grace of God today?

Lord, thank You for giving me Your amazing grace!

TWILIGHT YEARS

> *Let us hold tightly without wavering to the hope we*
> *affirm, for God can be trusted to keep his promise.*
> HEBREWS 10:23 NLT

In 2018, Luis Palau was diagnosed with stage four lung cancer. In an interview with *Christianity Today*, he said, "Every campaign, I always talked about heaven. So, to me, it is as real as flying to New York, only better. But the fact is that Satan attacks, and he'll use all his stratagems to make you feel guilty or lose faith or despair. Be ready for that. I went back to Hebrews 8, 9, and 10. . . . Go back to that. Don't read too many other books about heaven. Just read what the Bible says. Underline those passages. Take it to heart. Make notes to yourself that the One who is seated in heaven covered all your sins. Don't let Satan lie to you that some sins are unforgiven. They're all forgiven. They're all cleansed."

Whether you have a matter of days or possibly years of life ahead of you, your sins have been covered by the perfect sacrifice. Live in the freedom that comes with forgiveness—and expresses itself through love for God and others.

> *Lord, let me live in faith and die in the*
> *knowledge that Your sacrifice is enough.*

PILLAR FOR CENTURIES

*All hard work brings a profit, but mere
talk leads only to poverty.*
PROVERBS 14:23 NIV

In AD 429, North Africa was invaded by the Vandals, a Germanic people. Displaced natives flooded the handful of fortified cities, including Augustine's headquarters of Hippo. Seventy-six years old at the time, he tended to the people who had fled their homes. In the third month of the siege of Hippo, Augustine died of a fever.

Augustine left an incredible legacy, including books such as *Confessions* and *The City of God*, which are still read today. Some scholars say his theology was a main pillar on which the church was built for the next thousand years.

Throughout the generations, only a handful of people rise to the prominence of an Augustine. Few of us will be remembered ten years after our deaths, let alone a thousand. But in our own God-given times and ways, we should do what we can to "contend for the faith," as Jude 3 says. God calls each of us to be hardworking and diligent in His service, no matter what situation we find ourselves in.

Today, consider the example of Saint Augustine, who pursued excellence in every endeavor of life.

*Father, make me a dedicated and disciplined
worker in every aspect of my life.*

LIFE WORTH LIVING

*For whether we live, we live unto the Lord; and
whether we die, we die unto the Lord: whether
we live therefore, or die, we are the Lord's.*
ROMANS 14:8 KJV

Charles Haddon Spurgeon spent thirty-eight years as pastor of London's Metropolitan Tabernacle, growing the congregation from hundreds to thousands. And while he did his part well, Spurgeon acknowledged that it was God who gave the increase.

"The life of Jonah cannot be written without God; take God out of the prophet's history, and there is no history to write," Spurgeon said. "This is equally true of each one of us. Apart from God, there is no life, nor thought, nor act, nor career of any man, however lowly or however high. Leave out God, and you cannot write the story of anyone's career. . . . I believe that, in a man's life, the great secret of strength, and holiness, and righteousness, is the acknowledgment of God."

Will you acknowledge God's role in your story today? Thank Him for your blessings. Lean on Him when you struggle. Meditate on His Word and introduce others to His glory. That, according to C. H. Spurgeon, is the secret to a life worth living.

*Lord, keep me from thinking Your story is
about me when mine is all about You.*

HOME TO GLORY

The jailer. . .asked, "Sirs, what must I do to be saved?"
ACTS 16:29–30 NIV

After World War I, as the popularity of movies and radio increased, evangelist Billy Sunday drew smaller crowds. But he still received invitations to speak about Jesus, and he took them. He continued to share the truth of God's Word as aggressively as he had once played major league baseball.

Sunday once said, "I'm against sin. I'll kick it as long as I have a foot. I'll fight it as long as I have a fist. I'll butt it as long as I have a head. I'll bite it as long as I've got a tooth. And when I'm old and fistless and footless and toothless, I'll gum it till I go home to glory and it goes home to perdition."

Billy Sunday went home to glory in 1935, at the age of seventy-two. He had spoken before millions, and saw as many as three hundred thousand people turn their lives over to Jesus Christ. His final sermon, preached after Sunday had suffered a mild heart attack, was entitled, "What Must I Do to Be Saved?"

There's a lesson for all of us in Billy Sunday's life and death: keep fighting sin and sharing the gospel until the very end, when God calls us home to glory.

Father, please help me to finish well.

GIVE UP YOUR LIFE

> *"If you cling to your life, you will lose it; but if you give up your life for me, you will find it."*
> MATTHEW 10:39 NLT

Battling poor health and depression, Hudson Taylor still worked furiously in China. He also traveled to England and North America to recruit other missionaries. His service was costly: Taylor lost his first wife and four of his eight children. In 1900, he suffered a mental and physical breakdown.

You might ask yourself if the China Inland Mission was worth all that. The answer requires a larger biblical perspective—one that takes into account the eternal souls of millions of people.

Taylor's vision of reaching China is still alive and well. In 2015, OMF International, the former China Inland Mission, celebrated its one hundred and fiftieth anniversary. Its goal of sharing the gospel continues, but the organization has expanded into other countries in East Asia.

Other missionaries and evangelists—including Eric Liddell, Jim Elliot, Billy Graham, and Luis Palau—have cited Hudson Taylor's example as an inspiration to their own work.

So Hudson Taylor's sacrifices have benefited untold millions of people. What impact might your own daily sacrifices have for God's kingdom?

Father, take all of me. Mold me to be more like Christ that I may find the full life He offers.

FINAL PRAYER

*"If you remain in me and my words remain in you,
ask whatever you wish, and it will be done for you."*
JOHN 15:7 NIV

After more than a year in prison, Bible translator William Tyndale was officially condemned as a heretic and turned over to the secular authorities for execution. Given the opportunity to recant his belief that commoners should read God's Word in their own language, Tyndale refused.

In his final prayer, rather than asking God to spare him or to bring justice to his executioners, Tyndale called out in a loud voice, "Lord, open the king of England's eyes!" Then he was tied to a post, strangled, and set on fire.

But within four years of Tyndale's death, God answered his prayer. King Henry VIII commissioned a Bible to be published and read in churches. The basis of this "Great Bible" was largely Tyndale's own translation. Tyndale's Bible was also the foundation of the later King James Version, which retains 80 percent of his word choices.

Some of our prayers will not be answered in our lifetimes. But when our hearts are aligned with God's, He will do what is best, and at the best time. Trust His wisdom and goodness.

---

*Father, align my heart with Yours so my prayers are
answered—according to Your will and in Your time.*

ALL THE GOOD YOU CAN

For this is what the Lord has commanded us:
"I have made you a light for the Gentiles, that you
may bring salvation to the ends of the earth."
ACTS 13:47 NIV

By the end of his life, John Wesley had preached over 40,000 sermons, traveled roughly 250,000 miles, and given away at least 30,000 pounds. Today, the number of worldwide Methodists is around 40 million.

"I look upon the whole world as my parish," he once said, and by traversing Europe, the Atlantic, and the Americas to teach about Jesus, he lived out the words.

Though he gained worldwide fame for his life and work, John Wesley's approach was very simple: do all the good you can for Christ. In a sermon on money, he encouraged listeners to "employ whatever God has entrusted you with, in doing good, all possible good, in every possible kind and degree, to the household of faith, to all men."

We all have that opportunity. And God has placed each of us right where He wants us for carrying out His work. Whether you're at work or home or church or anywhere, use your time, energy, and resources to be a light to your world.

Father, help me to do good for You wherever I go today.

NOT RUSTING OUT

Do you see someone skilled in their work?
They will serve before kings; they will not
serve before officials of low rank.
PROVERBS 22:29 NIV

George Whitefield packed a lot of life into his fifty-five years. He helped ignite the First Great Awakening in the Colonies and England. He influenced the beginning of the Methodist church. He preached to millions, befriended Benjamin Franklin, and some say even set the stage for the American Revolution.

Frequently ill toward the end of his life, Whitefield refused to slow down. "I would rather wear out than rust out," he said.

Whitefield's final sermon, the day before he died, was preached in a field while he stood on a barrel. He reminded his hearers that good works will never get a person into heaven.

Though good works are insufficient to save, they are the natural response to being saved. When you work as hard as George Whitefield did for the glory of God, He will be well pleased in welcoming you to heaven.

How are you doing today? Wearing out for God? Or rusting out?

Father, forgive me when I get rusty in my
faith. I commit my work to Your glory.

ENDURANCE FOR GOOD

And as for you, brothers and sisters,
never tire of doing what is good.
2 THESSALONIANS 3:13 NIV

William Wilberforce fought slavery by making eloquent speeches, establishing a network of supporters, and consistently pursuing what his Christian faith told him was injustice. The battle lasted for decades.

During an abolition speech in 1789, Wilberforce said, "I mean not to accuse any one, but to take the shame upon myself, in common, indeed, with the whole parliament of Great Britain, for having suffered this horrid trade to be carried on under their authority. We are all guilty—we ought all to plead guilty, and not to exculpate ourselves by throwing the blame on others; and I therefore deprecate every kind of reflection against the various descriptions of people who are more immediately involved in this wretched business."

Though the slave trade was abolished in the British Empire in 1807, much time would pass before slavery itself was outlawed. Days before Wilberforce's death in 1833, the Slavery Abolition Act had its final reading in the House of Commons and went into effect the following year.

In God's eyes, endurance—in the pursuit of good—is a virtue. Whatever He's called you to do, stay with it. . .and trust in His ultimate blessing.

Father, I pray for endurance to complete
the work You have called me to do.

HEROIC HERETIC

*"Everyone will hate you because of me, but the
one who stands firm to the end will be saved."*
MARK 13:13 NIV

John Wycliffe's legacy is inseparable from the Reformation. His drive brought the Bible to the masses and spread the idea that scripture is the ultimate authority on all matters of faith.

Before the printing press had been invented, Wycliffe developed a team of translators who produced hundreds of copies of the Bible and distributed them throughout Europe. Wycliffe himself died in 1384, before that Bible was finished—but his vision for an English translation in many ways changed the world.

Amazingly, thirty-one years after his death, John Wycliffe was officially branded a heretic by Catholic church leaders. His bones were dug up and burned and the ashes thrown into the river Swift. A later chronicler observed, "Thus the brook hath conveyed his ashes into Avon; Avon into Severn; Severn into the narrow seas; and they into the main ocean. And thus the ashes of Wycliffe are the emblem of his doctrine which now is dispersed the world over."

We may not see the work God does through us coming to fruition during our lifetimes. But we can be sure that, as we seek to do His will, we are part of His eternal plan.

*Lord, I submit my life, my work, my passions, and my
energy to You. Use me to make Your name great.*

SCRIPTURE INDEX

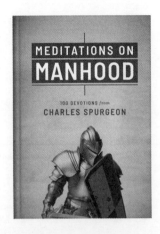